THiNK

STUDENT'S BOOK 1

A2

Herbert Puchta, Jeff Stranks & Peter Lewis-Jones

CAMBRIDGE
UNIVERSITY PRESS

CONTENTS

	FUNCTIONS & SPEAKING	GRAMMAR	VOCABULARY
Unit 1 **Having fun** p 12	Talking about routines and everyday activities Expressing likes and dislikes Giving warnings and stating prohibition	Present simple review *like + -ing* Adverbs of frequency	Hobbies **WordWise:** Collocations with *have*
Unit 2 **Money and how to spend it** p 20	Role play: Buying things in a shop Talking about what people are doing at the moment	Present continuous Verbs of perception Present simple vs. present continuous	Shops Clothes

	FUNCTIONS & SPEAKING	GRAMMAR	VOCABULARY
Unit 3 **Food for life** p 30	Talking about food Ordering a meal Apologising	Countable and uncountable nouns *a/an, some, any* *How much / many, a lot of / lots of* *too* and *(not) enough*	Food and drink Adjectives to talk about food **WordWise:** Expressions with *have got*
Unit 4 **Family ties** p 38	Talking about families Asking for permission	Possessive adjectives and pronouns *whose* and possessive *'s* *was* / *were*	Family members Feelings

	FUNCTIONS & SPEAKING	GRAMMAR	VOCABULARY
Unit 5 **It feels like home** p 48	Talking about events in the past Making suggestions Role play: Buying furniture for your youth club	Past simple (regular verbs) Modifiers: *quite, very, really*	Parts of a house and furniture Adjectives with *-ed* / *-ing* **WordWise:** Phrasal verbs with *look*
Unit 6 **Best friends** p 56	Saying what you like doing alone and with others Talking about past events Talking about friends and friendships	Past simple (irregular verbs) Double genitive Past simple questions	Past time expressions Personality adjectives

PRONUNCIATION	THINK	SKILLS	
/s/, /z/, /ɪz/ sounds	**Values:** Taking care of yourself **Self esteem:** Why it's good to have a hobby	Reading	Quiz: Do you take good care of yourself? Blog: So what do you do in your free time? Photostory: Olivia's new hobby
		Writing	Writing about routines
		Listening	Conversations about hobbies
Contractions	**Values:** Fashion and clothes **Train to Think:** Exploring numbers	Reading	Soap opera: Shopping Webchat: How not to spend money Culture: World markets
		Writing	An informal email to say what you're doing
		Listening	Shop dialogues
Vowel sounds: /ɪ/ and /iː/	**Values:** Food and health **Self esteem:** Being happy	Reading	Article: Food facts or food fiction? Blog: My brother's cooking Photostory: The picnic
		Writing	A paragraph about your favourite or least favourite meal
		Listening	Ordering food in a café
-er /ə/ at the end of words	**Values:** TV families **Train to Think:** Making inferences	Reading	Article: TV Families Article: The swimming pool heroes Culture: Around the world on Children's Day
		Writing	An invitation
		Listening	Why my family drive me mad
-ed endings /d/, /t/, /ɪd/	**Values:** Community spirit **Self esteem:** Feeling safe	Reading	Article: The Lego House Blog: Dad gets it right! (finally) Photostory: Hey, look at that guy!
		Writing	A blog post and a summary of a text
		Listening	What is home?
Stressed syllables in words	**Values:** Friendship and loyalty **Train to Think:** Making decisions	Reading	Article: Together Article: How we met Culture: Friendship myths
		Writing	An apology
		Listening	A story about Cristiano Ronaldo

A ALL ABOUT ME
Personal information

1 🔊 1.02 **Put the dialogue in order. Number the boxes. Listen and check.**

1	ALEX	Hi. I'm Alex.
	ALEX	I'm fourteen. How about you?
	ALEX	The United States.
	ALEX	Hello, Fabiola. Where are you from?
	ABIOLA	Me? I'm fourteen, too.
	FABIOLA	I'm from Italy. And you?
	FABIOLA	Hi, Alex. My name's Fabiola.
	FABIOLA	Cool! How old are you, Alex?

2 🔊 1.03 **Complete the dialogue with the phrases in the list. Listen and check.**

are | meet | this | too

ALEX	Fabiola – ¹_____ is my friend Ravi.
RAVI	Hi, Fabiola. Nice to ²_____ you.
FABIOLA	Nice to meet you, ³_____ , Ravi. And this is my friend: her name's Patrizia.
PATRIZIA	Hi, guys. How ⁴_____ you? I'm Patrizia. Patrizia Lambertucci.

3 **SPEAKING** **Imagine you are a famous person. Work in pairs, then groups.**

1 Tell your partner who you are.
2 Introduce your partner to others in the group.

Hi, I'm Ryan Gosling.

Hello, my name's Rihanna. And this is my friend, Barack Obama.

Nationalities and *be*

4 **Complete the names of the countries (add the consonants).**

1 __ __ a __ i __

2 __ __ e a __
__ __ i __ a i __

3 the __ e __ __ er-
__ a __ __ __ __

4 __ __ o __ o __ __ i a

5 I __ __ a __ __

6 __ e __ i __ o

7 __ u __ __ i a

8 __ __ __ a i __

9 __ u __ __ e __

10 the U __ i __ e __
__ __ a __ e __

11 A __ __ e __ __ i __ a

12 __ e __ __ i u __

Carlos

0 *He's Brazilian.*

Sandra

1 *She's* _____

Liam and Jane

2 _____

Natasha and Anna

3 _____

Ricardo

4 _____

Burcu

5 _____

Lotte

6 _____

Giovanni

7 _____

Andrea

8 _____

Raul and Luis

9 _____

5 What nationality are the people? Write the sentences.

6 ◀)) 1.04 Complete the dialogue using the correct forms of the verb *to be*. Then listen and check.

FABIOLA So, Ravi – where ⁰ _are_ you from?

RAVI Me? I ¹ _____ from Britain. Alex here ² _____ from the United States, but I ³ _____ British.

PATRIZIA But, ⁴ _____ your name British?

RAVI Oh, good question. Well, no it ⁵ _____ . My parents ⁶ _____ from India and so my name ⁷ _____ from India too. But my sister Anita and I were both born here, so we ⁸ _____ 100% British.

FABIOLA That ⁹ _____ cool. I think your name ¹⁰ _____ really nice.

RAVI Thank you! And you two, ¹¹ _____ you both Italian?

PATRIZIA That ¹² _____ right. But we ¹³ _____ not from the same city. I ¹⁴ _____ from Milan and Fabiola ¹⁵ _____ from Bari. We ¹⁶ _____ students at the language school here.

Names and addresses

7 ◀)) 1.05 Ravi phones for a taxi. Listen and complete the information.

COOPER'S TAXIS

Booking form

Taxi for	¹
Going to	²
Pick up at	³ am/pm
From	⁴ Street
Number of passengers	⁵

8 ◀)) 1.06 Now listen to a phone call. Correct each of these sentences.

0 Alex phones Patrizia.
   No – Patrizia phones Alex.

1 They met last Wednesday.

2 There's a party at Patrizia's place next Friday.

3 The party starts at seven thirty.

4 Patrizia lives at 134 Markam Avenue.

5 Her phone number is 0788 224 234.

B WHAT'S THAT?

Things in the classroom

1 Look at the pictures. Write the correct number next to each word.

board ☐   book ☐   CD ☐   chair ☐   desk ☐   floor ☐

pen ☐   pencil ☐   ruler ☐   window ☐   door ☐   notebook ☐

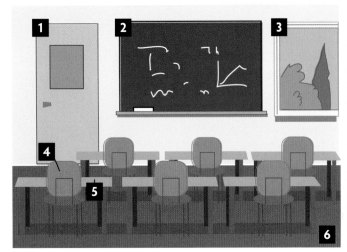
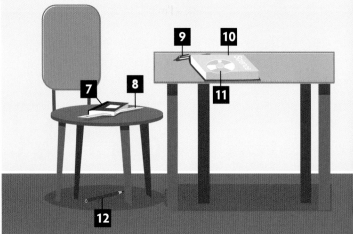

Prepositions of place

2 Look at the pictures. Complete each sentence with a preposition from the list (you will use some words more than once).

on | between | in | under | in front of | behind

0 The notebook is ___*on*___ the chair.

1 The pencil is _____ the floor.

2 The pencil is _____ the chair.

3 The book is _____ the desk.

4 The pen is _____ the book.

5 The ruler is _____ the notebook.

6 The board is _____ the door and the window.

7 The book is _____ the pen.

Classroom language

3 🔊 1.07 Complete each sentence with a word from the list. Listen and check.

ask | again | mean | hand | don't
page | me | say | spell | understand

1 Excuse _____ .

2 Can I _____ a question, please?

3 Can you say that _____ , please?

4 How do you _____ *cansado* in English?

5 Open your books at _____ 21.

6 Put your _____ up if you know the answer.

7 Sorry, I _____ know.

8 Sorry, I don't _____ .

9 What does this word _____ ?

10 Excuse me. How do you _____ that word?
    Is it T-I-R-E-D or T-Y-R-E-D?

4 🔊 1.08 Use one of the sentences in Exercise 3 to complete each mini-dialogue. Listen and check.

1 TEACHER   Good morning, everyone.
   STUDENTS   Good morning.
   TEACHER   OK. Let's start. _____

2 TEACHER   So, Michael, what's the answer?
   MICHAEL   _____
   TEACHER   That's OK. What about you, Susie?

3 STUDENT   _____ ,
              Mrs McFarlane. I've got a question.
   TEACHER   Yes, what is it?
   STUDENT   _____ : 'fascinating'?
   TEACHER   It means: 'very, very interesting'.

5 🔊 1.09 Put the lines in order to make a dialogue. Listen and check.

☐ A E-N-O-U-G-H.

☐ A No, that's completely wrong!

☐ 1 A How do you think you spell the word 'enough'?

☐ A No, that's really how you spell it.

☐ B OK, how do you spell it, then?

☐ B Oh. Let me think. Is it E-N-U-F-F?

☐ B You're kidding!

6 **SPEAKING** Work in pairs. Think of a word in English. Can your partner spell it?

> How do you spell 'awful'?   A-W-F-U-L.

> That's right.

Object pronouns

7 Complete each sentence with the correct pronoun.

0 She's a good teacher – we like ___*her*___ a lot.

1 My pens are under your desk. Can you get _____ , please?

2 I've got a new book – I'm going to read _____ this afternoon.

3 Sorry, can you speak more loudly? I can't hear _____ .

4 I really can't do this homework – can you help _____?

5 He doesn't understand so please help _____ .

6 We like our teacher. She gives _____ good marks!

this / that / these / those

8 Match the pictures and sentences.

1 What does this word mean?

2 What does that word mean?

3 These books are heavy.

4 Those books are heavy.

9 Complete the email by writing one word in each space.

To: shirley_2002@email.co.uk

Subject: Hello from Spain

Hi Shirley

I'm writing to you from Spain! My family and I ⁰ ___*are*___ on holiday here for two weeks. It's really nice here. Spanish people are very friendly but of course I don't speak Spanish so I don't ¹_____ when people talk to me. But a ²_____ of people here speak good English, so it's all OK.

Our hotel is great. ³_____ is a swimming pool downstairs and I swim there every day before breakfast. But of course I have breakfast late – usually nine o'clock! And it's always really good – the orange juice is delicious and I usually eat ham and eggs, too. Breakfast is my favourite meal – I love ⁴_____ .

So, ⁵_____ are you? I hope you are enjoying your holidays, too. I want to buy a present for you here in Spain. ⁶_____ would you like? ⁷_____ you like Spanish music? Write and tell ⁸_____ , OK?

Have a good time and write soon.

Love

Howard

A

Ditch

B

C

D

C ABOUT TIME
Days and dates

1 🔊 1.10 Listen and (circle) the correct information.

OLIVER	Hi, Shona. Why are you so happy today?
SHONA	Because it's the ¹*21st / 22nd / 23rd* February.
OLIVER	And what's special about that date?
SHONA	It's my birthday!
OLIVER	Really! Happy birthday, Shona.
SHONA	Thanks. I'm ²*12 / 13 / 14* today.
OLIVER	Lucky you!
SHONA	When is your birthday, Oliver?
OLIVER	It's in ³*August / September / October*.
SHONA	What date?
OLIVER	The ⁴*11th / 12th / 13th*. I think it's on a ⁵*Tuesday / Thursday / Friday* this year.

2 🔊 1.11 Complete the names of the days and months. Listen and check.

DAYS
1 M o n d a y
2 T _ _ sd _ _ _
3 W _ _ n _ d _ _
4 _ h u _ _ _ _ _ y
5 F _ _ _ _ _ _
6 S _ _ _ r _ _ y
7 S _ _ _ _ _ _

MONTHS
1 J _ _ _ u _ _ y
2 F _ bru _ _ _ _
3 M _ _ _ _ h
4 _ p _ _ l
5 M _ _ _
6 J _ _ _ _
7 J _ _ y
8 A _ _ u _ _
9 S _ _ _ _ _ mber
10 O _ _ _ _ _ er
11 _ _ _ vem _ _ _ _
12 D _ _ _ _ _ _ _ _

3 Draw lines to match the numbers and the words.

first	22nd
second	3rd
third	12th
fourth	4th
fifth	15th
twelfth	2nd
fifteenth	5th
twentieth	31st
twenty-second	1st
thirty-first	20th

4 🔊 1.12 How do you say these numbers? Listen and check.

7th | 11th | 14th | 19th | 23rd | 28th | 30th

5 🔊 1.13 Listen and write the people's birthdays.

1 *4th August*   2 _____

3 _____   4 _____

5 _____   6 _____

6 SPEAKING Walk around the classroom. Ask and answer questions. Whose birthday is close to your birthday?

When's your birthday?   *It's on 17th March.*

My day

7 Put the pictures in the order you do them.

I go to school.

I get home.

I go to bed.

I have dinner.

I have breakfast.

I get up.

I do my homework.

I have lunch.

8 Look at the sentences in Exercise 7. Write them in the correct column <u>for you</u>.

Morning	Afternoon	Evening
I get up.		

9 Match the clocks and the times.

1 It's half past eight.	5 It's eight o'clock.
2 It's quarter past three.	6 It's quarter to eight.
3 It's eleven o'clock.	7 It's ten to one.
4 It's six o'clock.	8 It's twenty past ten.

A 2

I _get home._

B

I _____

C

I _____

D

I _____

E

I _____

F

I _____

G

I _____

H

I _____

LOOK!

midday to midnight = pm
midnight to midday = am
12 am = midnight
12 pm = midday

1 am = 1 o'clock in the early morning
1 pm = 1 o'clock in the afternoon

10 🔊 1.14 Listen to Leah. Write about her day under the pictures in Exercise 9.

11 **SPEAKING** Work in pairs. Talk about your day.

I get up at half past seven.

I have lunch at twelve o'clock.

D MY THINGS
My possessions

1 Read Chloës's blog and tick (✓) the photos of the things she has got.

2 Work in pairs. How many things about Chloë can you write in each list?

PERSONAL POSSESSIONS: <u>TV</u>, <u>laptop</u>, _____, _____, _____, _____

PETS: <u>cat</u>, _____, _____,

have got

3 Complete the table with *have*, *has*, *haven't* or *hasn't*.

Positive	Negative
I've (have) got a dog.	I haven't (have not) got a cat.
You ^{1}_____ (have) got a dog.	You ^{5}_____ (have not) got a cat.
He's (has) got a dog.	He hasn't (has not) got a cat.
She ^{2}_____ (has) got a dog.	She ^{6}_____ (has not) got a cat.
We ^{3}_____ (have) got a dog.	We ^{7}_____ (have not) got a cat.
They ^{4}_____ (have) got a dog.	They ^{8}_____ (have not) got a cat.

Questions	Short answers
Have I got a pet?	Yes, you have. / No, you haven't.
^{9}_____ you got a pet?	Yes, I ^{13}_____ / No, I ^{14}_____
Has he got a pet?	Yes, he has / No, he hasn't.
^{10}_____ she got a pet?	Yes, she ^{15}_____ / No, she ^{16}_____
^{11}_____ we got a pet?	Yes, we ^{17}_____ / No, we ^{18}_____
^{12}_____ they got a pet?	Yes, they ^{19}_____ / No, they ^{20}_____

4 Complete the sentences with *have*, *has*, *haven't* or *hasn't* so they are true for you.

1 I _____ got a tablet.
2 My dad _____ got a computer.
3 I _____ got a dog.
4 My best friend _____ got a brother.
5 I _____ got a TV in my bedroom.
6 My mum _____ got a car.

5 **SPEAKING** Walk around the classroom. Find someone who has got ...

1 a red bike
2 a cat and a dog
3 an English dictionary
4 an email address
5 two brothers or sisters
6 a smart phone
7 an unusual pet
8 a house with a garden

> *Have you got a bike?*   *Yes, I have.*

> *What colour is it?*

WELCOME!

Hi, my name's Chloë,

I've got a bike – it's really my favourite thing!

I haven't got a pet but I'd love a cat or maybe something unusual like a lizard.

I haven't got a smart phone. I want one for my next birthday.

I've got an MP3 player and I've got a tablet. I haven't got a laptop. My dad's got one and I sometimes use that.

I've got a TV in my bedroom. And I've got a camera, a small one but it's nice.

I'm a very lucky girl.

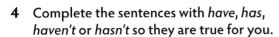

I like and *I'd like*

6 **Match the pictures and the sentences.**

 A ☐

 B ☐

 C ☐

 D ☐

1 I like apples!   3 I'd like six apples.
2 I'd like a hot shower!   4 I like hot showers.

7 🔊 1.15 **Complete with *I like* or *I'd like*. Listen and check.**

0 A What's your favourite food?
   B _*I like*_ curry best.

1 A Can I help you?
   B Yes, _____ a kilo of oranges.

2 A _____ an ice cream, please.
   B Chocolate or strawberry?

3 A What do you want to watch?
   B Well, _____ films, so can we watch a film, please?

4 A _____ cycling. Do you?
   B Not much. I think running's better.

5 A Do you want pizza or lasagne?
   B Well, pizza's my favourite food – but today, _____ lasagne, please!

8 **Complete with the words in the list.**

banana | orange juice | tuna | biscuit

> **Picnic Box**
> Sandwiches:
> cheese or ¹ _____
> Desserts:
> cake or ² _____
> Fruit:
> apple or ³ _____
> Drinks:
> water or ⁴ _____

9 🔊 1.16 **Listen to the dialogue. What does Max choose for his lunch? ⃝Circle the food above.**

10 🔊 1.16 **Write the questions in the spaces to complete part of the dialogue. Listen again and check.**

What fruit would you like?
Have you got bananas?
What would you like for lunch today?
Would you like a tuna sandwich or a cheese sandwich?

DINNER LADY	Hi, Max. ¹_____
MAX	I'd like a picnic box, please.
DINNER LADY	²_____
MAX	A cheese sandwich, please.
DINNER LADY	³_____
MAX	⁴_____
DINNER LADY	Yes, we have.
MAX	A banana, please.

11 **SPEAKING** **Work in pairs. Make a picnic box for your partner. Ask and answer questions.**

What would you like for ... ?

Would you like a ... or ... ?

1 HAVING FUN

OBJECTIVES

FUNCTIONS: talking about routines and everyday activities; expressing likes and dislikes; giving warnings and stating prohibition

GRAMMAR: present simple review; *like + -ing*; adverbs of frequency

VOCABULARY: hobbies; collocations with *have*

A

B

C

E

F

G

D

H

READING

1 Match the activities in the list with the photos. Write 1–8 in the boxes.

1	sleeping	5	reading
2	doing homework	6	dancing
3	playing football	7	tidying up
4	studying	8	singing

2 Are these activities fun? Write *always*, *sometimes* or *never*.

1 Sleeping is _____ fun.

2 Doing homework is _____ fun.

3 Playing football is _____ fun.

4 Studying is _____ fun.

5 Reading is _____ fun.

6 Dancing is _____ fun.

7 Tidying up is _____ fun.

8 Singing is _____ fun.

3 **SPEAKING** Work in groups of three and compare your ideas from Exercise 2.

I think dancing is always fun.

I think it's sometimes fun.

4 **SPEAKING** Think of more activities and say what you think.

Riding a bike is always fun.

Doing housework is never fun.

5 **◀)) 1.17** Read and listen to the quiz. Match the pictures with the questions in the quiz. Write 1–7 in the boxes.

Do you take good care of yourself?

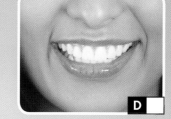

D

Does your teacher give you a lot of homework? Do your parents always want your bedroom tidy? School work, housework; life's not always easy. There are a lot of things to do and there isn't always time to do it all. But in your busy life it's important to think about yourself. It's important to do things you like, things that make you happy. Everyone needs fun.

So take our quiz and find out. Do you take good care of yourself?

4 How many hours do you sleep a night?
a) nine to ten hours
b) about eight
c) less than eight

5 Do you like exercise?
a) Yes, exercise is fun.
b) It's OK.
c) No. It's really boring.

1 Do you smile a lot?
a) Yes, I smile all the time.
b) I only smile when I'm happy.
c) My best friend says I don't smile very often.

A

6 Do you like puzzles and crosswords?
a) I love them.
b) They're OK.
c) I don't really like them. They're boring.

E

2 How many hobbies do you have?
a) I've got lots of hobbies.
b) One or two.
c) I don't have any hobbies.

B

F

G

3 When do you relax?
a) In the morning, afternoon and in the evening.
b) I relax when I have time.
c) I never relax. I'm always busy.

C

7 Which of these things do you do most?
a) Talk with friends and family.
b) Meet friends online.
c) Watch TV and play computer games.

■ THINK VALUES ■

Taking care of yourself

1 **Which questions in the quiz tell us that these things are important for us?**

a [7] Being with people
b [ ] Enjoying exercise
c [ ] Sleep
d [ ] Getting rest
e [ ] Giving your brain exercise
f [ ] Being positive
g [ ] Having interests

YOUR SCORE:

Mostly As: You take good care of yourself. You know how to have fun and enjoy life.

Mostly Bs: You take care of yourself OK, but can you do more? Try and find more time for yourself.

Mostly Cs: You don't take good care of yourself. Try and have more fun.

2 [SPEAKING] **Compare your ideas with a partner.**

Question 7 shows us that being with people is important.

GRAMMAR
Present simple review

1 Complete the sentences with the words in the list. Check your answers in the quiz on page 13.

~~relax~~ | do | does | don't | says

0   I never __relax__ .
1   My best friend _____ I don't smile very often.
2   I _____ really like them.
3   _____ your teacher give you a lot of homework?
4   _____ you like exercise?

2 Look at the sentences in Exercise 1 and the table. Complete the rule with *do*, *does*, *don't* or *doesn't*.

Positive	Negative
I **like** milk.	I **don't like** milk.
You **like** milk.	You **don't like** milk.
He/She/It **likes** milk.	He/She/It **doesn't like** milk.
We **like** milk.	We **don't like** milk.
They **like** milk.	They **don't like** milk.

Questions	Short answers	
Do I **like** milk?	Yes, you **do**.	No, you **don't**.
Do you **like** milk?	Yes, I **do**.	No, I **don't**.
Does he/she/it **like** milk?	Yes, he/she/it **does**.	No, he/she/it **doesn't**.
Do we **like** milk?	Yes, we **do**.	No, we **don't**.
Do they **like** milk?	Yes, they **do**.	No, they **don't**.

RULE: Use the present simple for things that happen regularly or that are always true.

In positive sentences:
* with *I, you, we* and *they*, use the base form of the verb.
* with *he, she* and *it*, add -*s* (or -*es* with verbs that end -*s*, -*sh*, -*ch*, -*x*, or -*z*).

In negative sentences:
* with *I, you, we* and *they*, use [1]_____ .
* with *he, she* and *it*, use [2]_____ .

In questions:
* with *I, you, we* and *they*, use the auxiliary [3]_____ .
* with *he, she* and *it*, use the auxiliary [4]_____ .

3 Complete the sentences. Use the present simple of the verbs.

0   I _don't like_ (not like) roller coasters. I _get_ (get) really scared on them.
1   My dad _____ (not sleep) a lot. He only _____ (need) five or six hours.
2   A _____ you _____ (study) English?
    B   Yes, I _____ .
3   My dad _____ (cook) really well but he says he _____ (not enjoy) it.
4   A _____ your sister _____ (play) in the school football team?
    B   No, she _____ .
5   My grandparents _____ (not like) travelling. They _____ (prefer) to stay at home.
6   My brother _____ (watch) TV all day. He _____ (not do) anything else.

Workbook page 10

Pronunciation
/s/, /z/, /ɪz/ **sounds**
Go to page 120.

VOCABULARY
Hobbies

1 Complete the phrases with the words in the list.

~~play~~ | write | keep | take | be | collect

0   to _play_ an instrument
1   to _____ in a club
2   to _____ a blog
3   to _____ photos
4   to _____ a pet
5   to _____ things

2 **SPEAKING** Work in pairs. Ask questions about the hobbies in the pictures.

Do you play an instrument?   *What do you play?*

Do you collect something? What ...?

Workbook page 12

YOUTH CLUB
NAME: Peter Summers
ADDRESS: 51 Willow Avenue
PHONE: 07734 384 587
MEMBERSHIP NUMBER: 09173

LISTENING

1 🔊1.20 **Listen to the conversations. Match each one with a picture.**

2 🔊1.20 **Listen again. Complete the sentences with the names in the list.**

~~Tom~~ | Carla | Lisa | Lisa's dad | James | James's mum

0 _____Tom_____ has got a headache.
1 _____ wants to join a football club.
2 _____ doesn't have time to relax.
3 _____ thinks music is good for relaxing.
4 _____ wants to be a famous piano player.
5 _____ thinks football is for boys.

▋THiNK SELF-ESTEEM▋

Why it's good to have a hobby

1 **Circle** the person from Listening Exercise 1.
I think it's good to have a hobby because …
1 you can make new friends.
   A Carla   B Lisa   C James
2 it helps you relax.
   A Carla   B Lisa   C James
3 you can discover you have new talents.
   A Carla   B Lisa   C James

2 **Copy the diagram into your notebooks and complete it with the hobbies in the list.**

playing the piano | joining a tennis club
collecting stamps | writing a blog
dancing | cooking | watching TV
playing online games | taking photos

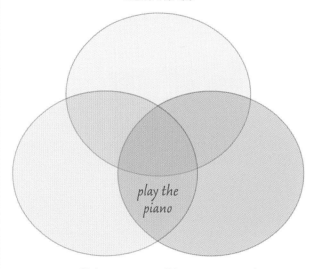

Make friends

play the piano

Relax   *Discover your talents*

3 **SPEAKING** **Work in pairs. Compare diagrams with your partner.**

> *Playing the piano is good. It helps you to relax.*

4 **What hobbies have you got? Think about why they are good for you. Make notes.**

5 **Tell your partner about your hobbies.**

> *I dance. I'm not very good but it helps me to relax.*

READING

1 **Read the blog and answer the questions.**

1 How many people like collecting things?
2 Who has got the strangest hobby?

So what do you do in your free time?

OK, we know you all like watching TV and playing computer games but we want to know some of the other things you do when you've got some free time. Write us a line or two and let us know.

Posted on January 22

NATHAN
I love collecting autographs of my friends and family. Now I want to get some from some famous people.

CHLOE
I enjoy lying on my back and looking at the clouds. I try to find different shapes in them. It's really relaxing and I occasionally fall asleep doing it.

IZZY
Once a week my granddad takes me out for a milkshake. I love listening to his stories. It's the best.

ADAM
I can't stand walking to school so I sometimes invent little games to help pass the time. For example I try to think of an animal, or football team or city for every letter of the alphabet.

LIZ
I like doing my homework as soon as I get home from school. Is there something wrong with me?

REBECCA
I really like going for a walk on my own in the forest near our house. There's always something interesting to see and I never get bored.

LEWIS
I collect bottle tops. I always take one home every time I go to a restaurant.

DYLAN
I like watching the news on TV. I watch it every day. My friends think I'm weird.

KUBA
I hate being on my own. So when I am by myself I usually start talking to my imaginary friends. But don't tell anyone!

JASMINE
I rarely get bored but if I do I just go to the library and get a book to learn about something new. It works every time.

DAISY
I like writing poems. I often write a poem when I've got nothing to do.

2 **Read the sentences. Which of the people above do you think is saying each one?**

0 A country that starts with R? Easy: Russia. — *Adam*

1 Have you got a book about birds? _____

2 Tell me more, please! _____

3 Can you write your name for me in my book? _____

4 Sorry, I can't come to the park now. I want to finish my maths. _____

5 Hey, that one looks just like a cow. _____

GRAMMAR
like + -ing

1 **Look at the sentences from the blog on page 16. Draw ☺ or ☹ next to each one.**

1 I love collecting autographs. _____
2 I can't stand walking to school. _____
3 I hate being on my own. _____
4 I like writing poems. _____

2 **Use the sentences in Exercise 1 to complete the rule.**

> **RULE:** Use the ¹_____ form of the verb after verbs which express likes and dislikes, e.g. *like, love, hate, enjoy, can't stand.*
> - To make this form add ²_____ to the base verb.
> - If the verb ends in -*e*, drop the final -e (e.g. *live – living*).
> - If a short verb ends in a consonant + vowel + consonant, we usually double the final consonant before adding the -*ing* (e.g. *swim – swimming*).

3 **Complete the sentences. Use the -*ing* form of the verbs in the list.**

~~run~~ | visit | swim | eat | ride | talk

0 I hate *running* to catch the bus to school.
1 My mum and dad enjoy _____ in nice restaurants.
2 My brother can't stand _____ on the telephone.
3 They quite like _____ in the sea when it's warm.
4 Donna really likes _____ her horse.
5 We love _____ new places on holiday.

4 **WRITING What about you? Write two or three sentences about yourself.**

Adverbs of frequency

5 **Complete the diagram with the words in the list.**

always | occasionally | never | often

6 **Complete the sentences so they are true for you.**

1 I _____ do my homework when I get home.
2 I _____ write 'thank you' cards for my presents.
3 I am _____ late for school.
4 I _____ watch TV in the mornings.
5 Mum is _____ angry if I don't tidy my room.
6 I _____ turn off the lights when I leave the room.

7 **Complete these sentences from the blog on page 16. Check your answers and complete the rule.**

1 _____ _____ _____ my granddad takes me out for a milkshake.
2 I watch it (the TV news) _____ _____ .

> **RULE:** Words like *sometimes, never, always* come ¹*before / after* the verb **to be** but ²*before / after* other verbs.
> Phrases like *every day* or *twice a week* can come at the beginning or at the end of a sentence.

8 **Write down things you do …**

every day: *I give my mum a kiss every day.*
three times a week: _____
once a year: _____

9 **SPEAKING Work in small groups. Compare your answers to Exercises 6 and 8.**

> How often do you go to the cinema?

> I go once a month …

Workbook page 11

WRITING
Your routine
Complete the sentences so they are true for you.

1 I rarely _____ at the weekend.
2 I can't stand _____ .
3 I _____ three times every day.
4 I love _____ in August.
5 I never _____ when I'm tired.
6 I _____ once a week.
7 I occasionally _____ .
8 I enjoy _____ after school.

Adverbs of frequency

0%   100%

¹_____   rarely   ²_____   sometimes   ³_____   usually   ⁴_____

Olivia's new hobby

1 Look at the photos and answer the questions.

What do you think Olivia's hobby is?
Why does Ryan look worried?

2 ◀)) 1.21 Now read and listen to the photostory.
Check your answers.

LUKE Look. It's Olivia and Megan.
RYAN What are they up to?
LUKE I'm not sure what they're doing but
they're definitely having a good time.
RYAN Let's go and find out.

OLIVIA Hi, Ryan. Hi, Luke.
RYAN Hi, Olivia. So what are you two doing?
OLIVIA It's my new hobby. I take photos of Megan
reading a book in strange places.
LUKE Cool! Can I video you on my phone?
OLIVIA Of course you can. Come on.

LUKE This is great. I think I've got a new hobby
too – making videos.
RYAN Be careful, Luke. Don't push too hard.
OLIVIA That's right. Be careful.
MEGAN Don't stop, Luke. I'm having fun.

OLIVIA That's great, Megan.
MEGAN Hurry up. My arms are tired.
I need to have a rest.
OLIVIA Just a few more.
RYAN Look out, Olivia! You're very close
to the water.

DEVELOPING SPEAKING

3 Work in pairs. Discuss what happens next in the story. Write down your ideas.

We think Olivia falls in the water.

4 ▶️ **EP1** Watch to find out how the story continues.

5 (Circle) the correct word in each sentence.

0 Ryan (tries) / *doesn't try* to warn Olivia.

1 Ryan and Luke *help / don't help* her out of the water.

2 Olivia *cries / doesn't cry* when she falls into the water.

3 Olivia *laughs / doesn't laugh* when she sees her camera.

4 Her camera *is / isn't* broken.

5 Luke *tells / doesn't tell* them what the surprise is.

6 Luke *gives / doesn't give* Olivia the money.

PHRASES FOR FLUENCY

1 Find the expressions 1–5 in the photostory. Who says them? Match them to the definitions a–f.

0 (What are they) up to? *Ryan* [e]

1 Cool! _____ [ ]

2 Come on. _____ [ ]

3 That's right. _____ [ ]

4 Hurry up. _____ [ ]

5 Look out! _____ [ ]

a Be quick.   d Let's start.

b Correct.   e Doing.

c Be careful.   f Great.

2 Complete the conversation with the expressions in Exercise 1.

In the park

SARAH   Hi, Nancy. What are you ⁰ *up to* ?

NICOLE   Not a lot. Just walking. Are you here for a walk too?

SARAH   ¹ _____ . I'm a bit bored at home.

NICOLE   Me too. We can walk together, if you want.

SARAH   ² _____ ! Oh no – ³ _____ ! Mike Smith is coming. I don't like him!

NICOLE   ⁴ _____ – let's walk over here.

SARAH   I don't want him to see me. ⁵ _____ , Nancy!

WordWise
Collocations with *have*

1 Match the sentence parts from the story.

1 [ ] I'm not sure what they're doing

2 [ ] Don't stop, Luke.

3 [ ] You're really dirty. You need to go home

4 [ ] My arms are tired.

5 [ ] Olivia, I think you *have a problem.*

6 [ ] We're just *having dinner.*

a I'm *having fun.*

b I think your camera's broken.

c It's pizza. Would you like some?

d I need to *have a rest.*

e but they're definitely *having a good time.*

f and *have a shower.*

2 Ask and answer the questions in pairs.

1 Who do you have the most fun with?

2 Do you have a good time at school?

3 What do you do when you have a problem?

4 What time do you have dinner?

5 Do you have a rest after school?

6 When do you have a shower?

Workbook page 12 ➤

FUNCTIONS
Giving warnings and stating prohibition

1 Put the words in order to make sentences.

1 Dan / Be / careful   3 do / that / Don't

2 out / Lucy / Look   4 push / Don't / hard / too

2 Match the sentences in Exercise 1 with the pictures A–D.

2 MONEY AND HOW TO SPEND IT

OBJECTIVES

FUNCTIONS: buying things in a shop; talking about what people are doing at the moment

GRAMMAR: present continuous; verbs of perception; present simple vs. present continuous

VOCABULARY: shops; clothes

READING

1 ◀)1.22 Say these prices. Listen and check.

PRICE €1.49 **1**

£22.75 **2**

$249.00 **3**

£5.99 **4**

$8.25 **5**

£835.00 **6**

2 ◀)1.23 What are these objects? Match them with the prices in Exercise 1. Write 1–6 in the boxes. Listen and check.

3 **SPEAKING** Work in pairs. Discuss the following questions. Then compare your ideas with other students.

Which of the things in Exercise 2 do you …
1 think are cheap?
2 think are expensive?
3 think are fantastic?
4 dream about having?

4 Look at the picture on page 21. Answer these questions.
1 Who do you think the boy and girl are?
2 Do you think the girl likes the shirt?

5 ◀)1.24 Read and listen to the script from a soap opera and check your ideas.

6 Mark the sentences T (true) or F (false). Correct the false ones.
0 It's six o'clock on Friday afternoon.
   It's four o'clock on Friday afternoon.
1 Tom is deciding what to wear.
2 Maddy thinks yellow is a good idea.
3 Tom thinks he's good-looking.
4 Tom wants to buy expensive clothes.
5 Tom wants to be famous.

A ☐   B ☐   C ☐

D ☐   E ☐   F ☐

TOM	Hi, Maddy.
MADDY	Where are Mum and Dad?
TOM	They're out. At the supermarket, I think. They're doing some shopping or something.
MADDY	What are you doing?
TOM	Me? I'm looking for something.
MADDY	OK. What are you looking for?
TOM	A shirt. And some trousers. I'm going out. It's Friday and I have plans for tonight. So, I'm choosing my clothes.
MADDY	But it's only four o'clock.
TOM	I know. I need time to choose.
MADDY	Do you need any help? I can help you.
TOM	No. Well, maybe. OK, yes.
MADDY	Think about colours.
TOM	I'm thinking. I'm thinking about … yellow.
MADDY	Not a good idea.
TOM	Why not?
MADDY	Because yellow just isn't interesting.
TOM	But I like yellow. Like this.
MADDY	I'm trying to help you, Tom. And I'm telling you – don't wear a yellow shirt.
TOM	You're laughing. Why are you laughing at me?
MADDY	I'm not laughing at you. I'm laughing at the shirt. It looks terrible.
TOM	I need some new ideas.
MADDY	You're right. Look at this. Here, in this magazine. See this guy? He's wearing beautiful clothes.
TOM	Yes, but he's good-looking. And rich too, probably. I'm not good-looking.
MADDY	Yes, you are! But of course, I'm only saying that because you're my brother. OK, have you got your money?
TOM	Yes. Why?
MADDY	I want to take you to town – to a clothes shop and maybe a shoe shop, too.
TOM	That sounds great. Nothing expensive though.
MADDY	Don't worry. Nice clothes aren't always expensive. Come on.
TOM	You know, I dream about being famous one day and about having fantastic clothes. Do you dream about that too?
MADDY	Tom, I'm nine years old. I dream about ice cream.
TOM	OK, we can get ice cream after we buy the clothes.

■ THiNK VALUES ■

Fashion and clothes

1 How important are these for you? Give each one a number from 0 to 5 (0 = not important, 5 = very, very important).

Clothes – my values:

- [ ] I want to look cool.
- [ ] I want to feel comfortable.
- [ ] I always buy cheap clothes.
- [ ] I like buying designer clothes.
- [ ] I love wearing clean clothes.
- [ ] I like wearing bright colours.
- [ ] I always buy clothes in the same shops.

2 **SPEAKING** Work in pairs. Ask and answer questions.

How important is it for you to look cool?

Not very important. I have 3 points. What about you?

For me, it's very important. 5 points.

GRAMMAR
Present continuous

1 **Look at the examples of the present continuous. Then complete the rule and the table.**

1 They**'re doing** some shopping at the supermarket.
2 He**'s wearing** beautiful clothes.
3 Why **are** you **laughing** at me?
4 I**'m not laughing** at you, Tom.

> **RULE:** Use the present ¹_____ to talk about things that are happening at or around the time of speaking.
>
> Form the present continuous with the present simple of ²_____ + the *-ing* form (e.g. *running* / *doing* / *wearing*, etc.) of the main verb.

Positive	Negative
I'm (= I am) working.	I'm not working.
you/we/they're (¹_____) working.	you/we/they aren't working.
he/she/it's (is) working.	he/she/it ²_____ working.

Questions	Short answers
³_____ I working?	Yes, I am. No, I'm not.
⁴_____ you/we/they working?	Yes, you/we/they ⁶_____ . No, you/we/they ⁷_____ .
⁵_____ he/she/it working?	Yes, he/she/it ⁸_____ . No, he/she/it ⁹_____ .

2 **Complete the sentences. Use the present continuous of the verbs.**

0 Sorry, Jenny's not here. She *'s doing* (do) some shopping in town.
1 They're in the living room. They _____ (play) computer games.
2 My brother's in the garage. He _____ (clean) his bike.
3 Steven! You _____ (not listen) to me!
4 I can't talk now. I _____ (do) my homework.
5 It's 3–0! We _____ (not play) very well, and we _____ (lose)!
6 A _____ you _____ (watch) this programme?
   B No, I _____ . You can watch a different one if you want.
7 A What _____ you _____ (do)?
   B I _____ (try) to find some old photos on my computer.

Workbook page 18

VOCABULARY
Shops

1 **Write the names of the shops under the photos.**

newsagent's | chemist's | bookshop
clothes shop | shoe shop | department store
supermarket | sports shop

1 _____

2 _____

3 _____

4 _____

5 _____

6 _____

7 _____

8 _____

2 **SPEAKING** **Complete the sentences with the names of shops from Exercise 1. Then compare your ideas with other students.**

1 In my town there's a very good …
   It's called … It's good because …
2 I often go there because …
3 I never go into … because they don't interest me.
   I don't often go to … because …

> *In my town there's a very good clothes shop.*
> *It's good because the clothes aren't expensive.*

Workbook page 20

GRAMMAR
Verbs of perception

1 Look at the sentences from the script on page 21. Answer the questions.

1 *It looks terrible.* What is 'it'?
2 *That sounds great.* What is 'that'?

2 Match the verbs with the pictures. Then complete the rule.

1 look 2 sound 3 smell 4 taste

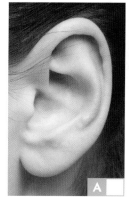
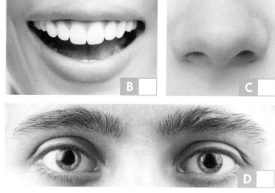

> **RULE:** Verbs of perception are used in the present ¹_____ when they are used to give an opinion.
>
> *The food* **tastes** *great.   That idea* **sounds** *good.   That pizza* **smells** *nice.   His new shirt* **looks** *awful!*
>
> The words after the verbs of perception are ²_____.

3 Match the responses (a–d) to the first parts of the conversations (1-4).

1 I'm going to the cinema. ☐
2 My mother's making pizzas. ☐
3 I'm wearing my new shoes. ☐
4 Don't you like the juice? ☐

a No. It tastes horrible!
b That sounds great.
c They smell fantastic.
d They look nice.

> Workbook page 19

LISTENING

1 🔊 1.25 Listen. What shop is each person in? Write numbers.

☐ bookshop   ☐ newsagent's
☐ clothes shop   ☐ sports shop

2 🔊 1.25 Listen again. What does each person want to buy?

1 _____   3 _____
2 _____   4 _____

FUNCTIONS
Buying things in a shop

1 Read the sentences from the listening. Mark them C (customer) or A (assistant).

0 Can I help you? A
1 Have you got … ? ☐
2 What size do you take? ☐
3 Can I try it/them on please? ☐
4 How much is it/are they? ☐
5 That's (twenty pounds) please. ☐
6 Have you got it/them in (blue)? ☐

2 🔊 1.26 Put the sentences in the correct order 1–9. Listen and check. Practise in pairs.

☐ A It's £75.00.
1 A Hello. Can I help you?
☐ A Great. So – that's £75, please!
☐ A Sorry, no. Only brown.
☐ A Yes, of course.
☐ B Can I try it on?
☐ B Very nice. I'll take it.
☐ B Yes, please. I like this jacket. Have you got it in black?
☐ B Oh, well, brown's OK. How much is it?

ROLE PLAY Buying clothes in a shop

Work in pairs. Student A: Go to page 127.
Student B: Go to page 128. Take two or three minutes to prepare. Then have two conversations.

■ TRAIN TO THiNK ■
Exploring numbers

1 You want to buy some new clothes. Here are some things you like. Answer the questions in pairs.

T-Shirt – £8.50   shoes – £12.75   jumper – £9.25
belt – £3   jacket – £35

1 Choose three things. How much do they cost?
2 You've got £30.00. Name three things you can buy.
3 You've got £75.00. Can you buy all five things?

2 **SPEAKING** Compare your ideas with a partner.

> **Pronunciation**
> Contractions
> **Go to page 120.** 🔊

VOCABULARY
Clothes

1 🔊 1.29 **Complete the names of the clothes. Listen and check.**

0 _b_ e _l_ _t_
1 __ __ e __ __ __
2 __ u __ __ e __
3 __ __ oe __
4 __ __ ai __ e __ __ __

5 __ oo __ __
6 __ a __ __ e __
7 __ __ i __ __
8 __ __ o __ __ __ __
9 __ __ ou __ e __ __ __

2 **Answer the questions.**

1 What are you wearing now?
2 What do you usually wear at the weekends?
3 What do you never wear?
4 What clothes do you really like / dislike buying?

3 **SPEAKING** Work in pairs. Ask and answer the questions in Exercise 2. Then work with another partner.

> I'm wearing a green shirt and jeans.

> I never wear shorts.

> Workbook page 20

READING

1 **Read the web chat. Answer the questions.**

Who …
1 is interested in the sky?
2 is probably in the kitchen?
3 has a problem?
4 is in front of a TV?
5 is surprising her parents?

2 **Think of three things you enjoy that don't need money. Write them down.**
going for a walk   watching TV

3 **SPEAKING** Work in pairs. Tell your partner your ideas. Listen to what your partner says. Are his/her ideas really things that don't need money? Say what you think.

> I like going for a walk. I also like watching TV.

> I like baking cakes.

> But you need money to buy ingredients!

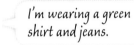

How not to spend money ✕

JollyMarie
5 June 2015

Wow! Problem. Not a lot of money right now and I don't want to spend it. I'm tired of spending money! So here I am at home and I'm thinking – what can I do that's free? (and fun lol)

👍 👎 LIKE · COMMENT · SHARE

goodgirl
an hour ago

I always go into town at the weekend – and I usually spend money! It's very easy to buy things if you go into a shopping mall or a street full of shops. So this weekend I'm staying at home. Right now I'm just reading a book – my parents can't believe it! lol

PeteJ
yesterday

I really like going to the cinema but it can be a bit expensive – especially because my friends and I often go for a pizza after the film. So tonight I'm watching a film on TV at home. I'm really enjoying it. And it's free! It's incredible how many good films there are on TV these days, too.

RonnieRaver
two days ago

It's funny, PeteJ – I'm just like you (going to the cinema, I mean). Right now, I'm not watching a film – I'm watching the stars! I've got a book about the sky and it's fantastic. I'm having a really good time here!

EllieParsons
two days ago

Oh JollyMarie, it's not such a problem. My friends and I often have a picnic on Sundays and I make the sandwiches the night before. So right now, it's Saturday night and I'm making sandwiches. hehehe

GRAMMAR
Present simple vs. present continuous

1 Look at the examples. Complete the rule.

present simple
I usually **watch** a film at the cinema.
I **make** the sandwiches the night before.
I always **go** into town.

present continuous
Right now, I'**m watching** a film.
It's Saturday night and I'**m making** sandwiches.
This weekend, I'**m staying** at home.

> **RULE:** Use the [1]_____ to talk about habits, routines and things which are generally or always true.
> Use the [2]_____ to talk about temporary things which are happening around the moment of speaking.

2 Match the sentences with the pictures. Write 1–4 in the boxes.

1 She sings well.
2 She's singing well.
3 He plays football.
4 He's playing football.

SINGING COMPETITION
1st PRIZE
AMANDA MARSHALL

> **LOOK!** These verbs are almost never used in the present continuous:
>
> believe | know | understand | mean
> remember | need | like | hate | want
>
> I **know** the answer. (Not: ~~I'm knowing the answer.~~)
> I **understand** the problem. (Not: ~~I am understanding the problem.~~)

3 Circle the correct options.

1 We *always wear* / *'re always wearing* a uniform to school.
2 Paula *wears* / *is wearing* black jeans today.
3 Come inside! It *rains* / *'s raining*.
4 It *rains* / *'s raining* a lot in February.
5 Dad *cooks* / *'s cooking* at the moment.
6 My mother *cooks* / *'s cooking* lunch every Sunday.
7 Steve's terrible! He *never listens* / *'s never listening* to the teacher!
8 Can you be quiet, please? I *listen* / *'m listening* to some music.

4 Complete the sentences. Use the present simple or present continuous form of the verbs.

0 Mandy usually ___*goes*___ (go) to school on her bike, but today she ___*is walking*___ (walk).
1 We _____ (have) science lessons three times a week. This week we _____ (learn) about trees.
2 Tom _____ (do) some shopping this afternoon. He _____ (want) to buy a new camera.
3 I _____ (know) her face, but I _____ (not remember) her name.
4 Alex _____ (not watch) the game tonight because he _____ (not like) football very much.
5 What _____ this word _____ (mean)? I _____ (not understand) it.

Workbook page 19

SPEAKING

1 Look at these photos. Who are the people in each one?

2 Work in pairs. Discuss the questions.

For each person, say …
* who they are.
* what they do.
* what they are doing.

> *It's Beyoncé. She's a …*
> *She's …*

Culture

1 Look at the photos. Name one or two things you can buy in each market.

- Where can you see stalls?
- Where can you see a canal?

2 ◀)1.30 Read and listen to the article. Match the photos with the places. Write the numbers 1–5 in the boxes.

A

World markets

Wherever you go in the world, you find shops and stores – but you can find wonderful markets in most cities, too. Here's a selection from five different countries.

B

1 The **Spice Bazaar** in **Istanbul** is popular with both tourists and people from Istanbul. There are lots of shops and stalls and they all sell many different kinds of spices, sweets or nuts. You can buy spices from a lot of countries (like Iran, China, Russia and of course Turkey), and the smells and colours are amazing.

2 **Khlong Lat Phli** is a very unusual market about 80 kilometres south of **Bangkok**, Thailand. Early every morning, hundreds of local people sell fruit and vegetables from their boats on the canals. It's not the only boat market in the country but it's a very popular tourist one.

3 Do you like fish? Then the **Tsukiji Market** in **Tokyo** is the right place for you. It is the biggest seafood market in the world, and

it never closes! It's very busy between the hours of 4.00 and 5.00 am, when people from the shops and restaurants in Tokyo buy the fresh fish that they need for the day. It is also very popular with tourists, but they can only visit the market later in the day, after the early morning buying and selling.

4 In **Madrid** there is a famous open-air market called **El Rastro**, which is open on Sunday mornings. There are over 1,000 stalls that sell many different things: books, CDs, paintings, antiques – beautiful old things. One of the streets sells only animals and birds. And of course visitors can stop to eat 'tapas' and get something to drink, and there are many street musicians with their guitars making music too.

C

5 **Portobello Road Market** in **London** is popular with tourists and with Londoners, too. You can find all kinds of bargains here. The market (in Notting Hill) has five different parts and you can buy new or second-hand things (like clothes) as well as fruit and vegetables, and antiques. It's very busy at the weekend.

D

E

3 VOCABULARY **There are eight highlighted words in the article. Match the words with these meanings. Write the words.**

0   big tables or small shops with an open front   *stalls*
1   not inside a building   _____
2   fish and other things to eat from the sea   _____
3   different or surprising   _____
4   small man-made rivers   _____
5   full of people   _____
6   liked by a lot of people   _____
7   things that you buy for a good, cheap price   _____

4 **Read the article again. Correct the information in these sentences.**

0   All the spices at the Istanbul Spice Bazaar are from Turkey.
    Not all the spices are from Turkey. You can buy spices from a lot of countries.
1   At Khlong Lat Phli, people sell spices from their boats.
2   The Tsukiji Market closes between four and five in the morning.
3   Tourists can go to the Tsukiji Market in the early morning.
4   You can't get food at El Rastro.
5   Portobello Road Market is very quiet on Saturdays.

SPEAKING

1 **Make sentences about the markets that are true for you. Use adjectives from the list, or other adjectives if you want.**

fantastic | interesting | fascinating
exciting | unusual | attractive

I think the ... market is fantastic / isn't very interesting because ...

2 **Work in groups. Compare your sentences and ideas.**

> *I think the Istanbul Spice market is fantastic because ...*

WRITING
An email to say what you're doing

1 **Read the email from Paul to his friend Lucy. Answer the questions.**

1   Where is Paul and what is he doing?
2   Where are his father and sister?
3   What is Paul's family watching tonight?

2 **How does Paul start his email? And how does he finish it? Complete the table with the words in the list.**

Dear | Love | Hello | See you soon | Best wishes

starting an email	ending an email
Hi (Lucy),	Hope you are OK.
1 _____ (Mike)	Bye
2 _____ (Mr Jones)	3 _____
	4 _____
	5 _____

3 **Look at paragraphs 1 and 2 of Paul's email. Match the functions with the paragraphs. Write a–d.**

Paragraph 1: _____ and _____ .
Paragraph 2: _____ and _____ .

a   saying what you are doing
b   talking about your plans
c   saying where you are
d   a description of the place where you are

4 **Tick (✓) the things Paul writes about in his email.**

1   what he likes about the city   ☐
2   when he is coming home   ☐
3   his plans for tonight   ☐
4   where he is staying   ☐
5   what his mother/father/sister are doing   ☐
6   how Lucy is   ☐

5 **Write an email to a friend (about 100–120 words). Imagine you are in a café or shop in a shopping centre. Use the example email and language above to help you.**

To: Lucy10@email.co.uk
Subject: Hello from Madrid!

Hi Lucy

(1) How are things with you? I'm in Madrid right now – we're here on holiday. Madrid is a really cool place. There are lots of great things to see and do here – shops, markets, and of course the football stadium! We're staying in a small hotel in the middle of Madrid, and it's really nice.

(2) I'm sitting in a café at the moment, in the middle of the city. I'm here with my mum and we're having a drink because it's really hot today! My father and my sister are at a market near here – they're looking for some shoes for my sister. Tonight we're watching a flamenco dancing show. I don't especially like dancing but all the family do, so … !

(3) OK my father and sister are coming back so I'm going now. Write soon and tell me how you are.

Hope you're OK.

Paul

CAMBRIDGE ENGLISH: Key

THiNK EXAMS

READING AND WRITING
Part 3: Multiple-choice replies

Workbook page 17

1 Complete the five conversations.
Choose the correct answer A, B or C.

0 What are you doing?
   A I play computer games.
   B I'm a doctor.
   C I'm trying to find my school bag. ✓

1 How often are you late for school?
   A on Mondays
   B about once a month
   C at ten o'clock

2 Does your brother go to your school?
   A Yes, he does go.
   B Yes, he goes.
   C Yes, he does.

3 What do you think of my new haircut?
   A It looks really good.
   B It's looking really good.
   C It sounds great.

4 Do you like doing puzzles?
   A Yes, I like.
   B Three times a week.
   C No, I can't stand them.

5 Do you live in a big town?
   A No, we aren't.
   B Yes, we do.
   C No, you don't.

Part 6: Word completion

Workbook page 43

2 Read the descriptions of clothes. What is the word
for each one? The first letter is already there. There
is one space for each other letter in the word.

0 You can wear this over your shirt when you go out.
   J a c k e t

1 Wear these shoes to play sport. t _ _ _ _ _ _ _ _ _

2 Put this on if it's cold. j _ _ _ _ _ _

3 Some boys wear trousers to school, other boys wear
   these. s _ _ _ _ _ _

4 You wear this around the top of your trousers.
   b _ _ _

5 A lot of teenagers wear these. j _ _ _ _ _

LISTENING
Part 1: Multiple-choice pictures

Workbook page 25

3 🔊 1.31 You will hear five short conversations.
There is one question for each conversation. For
each question, choose the right answer (A, B or C).

0 What are the girls talking about?

 A   B ✓   C

1 When does Oliver play tennis?

A   B C

2 Where is Brian?

A   B C

3 What is Molly's hobby?

A B   C

4 How much is the red jumper?

A B   C

TEST YOURSELF

UNITS 1 & 2

VOCABULARY

1 Complete the sentences with the words in the list. There are two extra words.

newsagent's | take | dress | club | write | plays | collects
sports shop | supermarket | jumper | shoe shop | belt

1 I want to _____ a blog about pop music.
2 If you're cold, why don't you put on a _____?
3 She _____ the guitar and the piano. She's really good at both.
4 I need to go to the _____ and buy some tennis balls.
5 My dad _____ old toy cars. He's just a big child!
6 You need some new boots. Let's go to the _____ .
7 I'm thinking about joining the golf _____ but it's very expensive.
8 Your trousers are falling down. You need a _____ .
9 Can you get some eggs and some milk when you go to the _____ , please?
10 I always _____ lots of photos when I travel.

`/10`

GRAMMAR

2 Complete the sentences with the words in the list.

's working | 're writing | works | plays | 're playing | write

1 My dad's a cook. He _____ at a restaurant in town.
2 I like poetry. I _____ at least five poems every week.
3 Mum's in her office. She _____ on something very important.
4 Paul's in a band. He _____ the drums.
5 Ian and Dan are on the computer. They _____ their blog.
6 Lucy and Rachel are in the garden. They _____ football.

3 Find and correct the mistake in each sentence.

1 I can't stand to eat carrots.
2 We don't playing very well today.
3 They doesn't like playing video games.
4 That sandwich is tasting very good.
5 Does you speak French?
6 He goes always swimming at the weekend.

`/12`

FUNCTIONAL LANGUAGE

4 Write the missing words.

1 A Be _____ ! It looks very dangerous.
  B Don't worry. I'm _____ fun.
2 A How _____ do you watch TV?
  B _____ day when I get home from school.
3 A Look _____ ! There's a dog coming.
  B And it _____ look happy. Let's run!
4 A Please _____ shout! The baby is asleep.
  B Oh, OK. I'm _____ .

`/8`

MY SCORE `/30`

22 – 30
10 – 21
0 – 9

OBJECTIVES

FUNCTIONS: apologising; talking about food; ordering a meal

GRAMMAR: countable and uncountable nouns; *a/an, some, any; How much / many, a lot of / lots of ; too* and *(not) enough*

VOCABULARY: food and drink; adjectives to talk about food; expressions with *have got*

A bread

READING

1 **What food and drink in the picture can you name? What food and drink do you know in English?**

2 **Make sentences that are true for you. Compare your ideas in class.**

	always often sometimes never	have … for	breakfast. lunch. dinner.
I			

3 **Look at the photos on page 31. Ask your teacher for the words you don't know. Then answer the questions.**

> *What's … in English?*

Can you think of a food that …

- comes from another country?
- has got a lot of vitamins?
- is very healthy?
- is unusual?
- is good for your hair and skin?

4 ◁》 **1.32 Read and listen to the article. Match the parts of the sentences.**

0	In Japan people think square watermelons	*e*
1	Bananas are a popular fruit because they	
2	In Iceland people don't like	
3	Honey is healthy and good	
4	Avocado is a dessert in	
5	Potato clocks are very popular in	
6	Sugar is not only in sweets. It's also in	

a 'normal' ice creams.
b Brazil.
c for our looks.
d West Africa.
e make very special presents.
f fruit.
g help us feel good.

5 **SPEAKING Work in pairs. Three of the 'food facts' in Exercise 4 are not true. Which ones do you think they are?**

> *I don't think that people give square watermelons as special presents in Japan.*

> *I think it's true that …*

> *Yes, you're right. I think so too. / No, I think that's impossible.*

> *What do you think about statement number …?*

> *I'm not sure. I think … Do you agree?*

> *Yes, I do. / No, I don't. I think …*

Food Facts or Food Fiction?

In Japan, square watermelons are very popular. People often buy them as presents. But these special fruits are of course very expensive. Round watermelons do not cost so much.

People all over the world love bananas. Food experts say that bananas contain a chemical that helps the body to produce serotonin. It's sometimes called the body's own 'happiness hormone'.

People in Iceland love eating unusual ice creams. There is pizza ice cream, sausage ice cream and even fish and chips ice cream, and they are all very popular. People eat them with a lot of ketchup. But you don't find any lemon or mango ice creams there. Icelanders just don't like them.

Honey is very healthy. It has got lots of vitamins. Some people say that honey makes us beautiful. They think it's good for the hair and the skin. Honey is also very special because it is the only food we eat that never goes off. We can eat 3,000- or 4,000-year-old honey!

The avocado is a fruit, not a vegetable. It comes from Central and South America originally, but now it also grows in other hot countries. Many people like avocados as a starter before their main meal. But how many people eat it as a dessert? Well, in Brazil, people eat avocado with ice cream and milk.

People in West Africa use a 'potato-clock' to tell the time. Every morning, they put exactly 7.5 kilos of potatoes in the clock. It looks like a big pot. They put it on the fire. They know that it takes two hours to cook the potatoes.

Everybody knows that fruit has got sugar in it. But how much sugar is there in a lemon? A lot. More than there is in a strawberry!

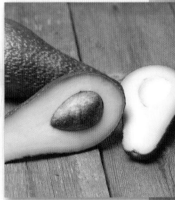

■ THiNK VALUES ■

Food and health

1 **Complete the five conversations. Choose the correct answer A, B or C.**

1 Do you want some ice cream?
   A No, thanks. Can I have an apple or a banana?
   B She's not hungry.
   C They're very good.

2 Have some water.
   A I drink it.
   B No, thanks, I'm not thirsty.
   C Look at them.

3 Would you like more chocolate?
   A It's over there.
   B Yes, I do.
   C I'd love some, but I'm trying not to eat too much.

4 Do you eat any vegetables?
   A I hate apples.
   B It's fast food.
   C No, I don't. I don't like them.

5 Have some biscuits.
   A Thanks, but one's enough for me.
   B You can have a banana.
   C I'm very healthy.

2 **SPEAKING Work in pairs. Compare your answers. Do the people care about healthy food?**

The person in number 1	doesn't want a ... likes ... never eats / drinks ...	He/She asks for ... He/She says ... He/She wants ...

I think he/she	cares about ... doesn't care about ...

VOCABULARY
Food and drink

1 🔊 1.33 **Write the names of the food under the pictures. Listen and check.**

1 _____ 2 _____ 3 _____ 4 _____ 5 _____

6 _____ 7 _____ 8 _____ 9 _____ 10 _____

2 **SPEAKING** **Work in pairs. Ask and answer questions to find out three things your partner likes and doesn't like.**

Workbook page 30

GRAMMAR
Countable and uncountable nouns

1 **Read the sentences. Then circle the correct words in the rule.**

1 Can I have a carrot? 2 I don't like rice.
3 I don't like peppers.

> **RULE:** Nouns that you can count (*one carrot, two carrots*, etc.) are ¹*countable / uncountable* nouns.
>
> Nouns you cannot count are ²*countable / uncountable* nouns. They have no plural forms.

2 **Look at the photos in Exercise 1. Which are countable and which are uncountable?**

a/an, some, any

3 **Complete the sentences with *a/an*, *some* and *any*. Then circle the correct words in the rule.**

1 A Would you like _____ water?
  B No, thanks. I've got _____ tea.
2 Can I have _____ apple or _____ banana?
3 Have _____ biscuits.
4 Are there _____ vegetables in the kitchen?
5 There isn't _____ milk in the fridge.

> **RULE:** Use *a/an* with ¹*singular / plural* countable nouns.
>
> Use *some* with ²*singular / plural* countable and uncountable nouns.
>
> Use *any* in questions and in ³*positive / negative* sentences.
>
> Use *some* in questions when offering or requesting something.

4 **Complete the sentences with *a/an*, *some* and *any*.**

1 A Would you like _____ vegetables?
  B No, thanks. I don't like _____ vegetables.
2 A I'd like _____ strawberries, please.
  B Strawberries? Yes, I think we have _____ .
3 I'd like _____ tomatoes.
4 I don't want _____ coffee.
5 Can I have _____ orange, please?
6 Do you want _____ sugar in your tea?

(how much) / (how) many / a lot of / lots of

5 **Look at the examples. Complete the rule.**

How much sugar is there in a lemon?	**How many** people eat avocado as a dessert?
I don't eat **much** chocolate.	We haven't got **many** apples.
Bananas have got **a lot of** sugar.	**A lot of** people like avocados.
Watermelons have got **lots of** water.	Honey has got **lots of** vitamins.

RULE: We typically use *(How) much* and *(How) many* in **questions** and **negative** sentences.

Use *many* with **plural** [1]_____ nouns and *much* with [2]_____ nouns.

Use *a lot of / lots of* with both **countable** and **uncountable** [3]_____ .

6 Circle the correct words in questions 1–6. Then match them with the answers a–f.

1 ☐ How *much / many* apples do you want?
2 ☐ How *much / many* sugar is there in an avocado?
3 ☐ Are there *much / many* boys in your class?
4 ☐ How *much / many* peppers are there?
5 ☐ How *much / many* time have you got?
6 ☐ Have you got *many / a lot of* homework?

a I think there are about five.
b Just one, please.
c Only 10 minutes.
d No, I haven't got any.
e I have no idea. I don't think it's a lot.
f Yes, there are 12, and 5 girls. **Workbook page 28**

LISTENING

1 🔊 1.34 Complete the menu with words from the list. Listen and check.

cheesecake | chips | tomato | onion rings | chicken spinach and mushroom | hot chocolate | fruit

BLUES CAFÉ MENU

OUR DELICIOUS STARTERS
[1]_____ soup
mushroom soup
[2]_____ omelette
ham and cheese omelette

LUNCH SPECIALS
steak
grilled [3]_____
pasta with tomatoes

SIDE DISHES
[4]_____
[5]_____
mixed salad

DESSERTS
yoghurt and strawberries
vanilla and chocolate ice cream
[6]_____

DRINKS
[7]_____ juices
mineral water
[8]_____
tea
coffee

2 🔊 1.35 Jane and Sam are in the Blues Café. Listen and find out who eats more. Listen again and complete the sentences below.

1 Jane wants the …
2 Sam orders …
3 He doesn't want …

3 🔊 1.35 Complete the sentences with *get, menu, drink, we'd, some* and *bill*. Then listen again and check.

Waiter: / Customer:

Can I help you? → [1]_____ like something to eat. Thanks.

Here's the [2]_____ .

What would you like to [3]_____ ? → An orange juice for me, please.

I'll be right back. ← And for me [4]_____ mineral water, please

What can I [5]_____ you? → I'd like the spinach and mushroom omelette.

Would you like a starter? → Yes, please. Can I have the … , please? / No, thanks.

Can we have the [6]_____ , please?

Of course. That's £ … . Here you are.

Thank you. Bye, bye / Thanks very much. ← Thank you. Bye.

4 **SPEAKING** Work in groups. One is the waiter, the others are customers. Order meals. Use the menu in Exercise 1 and the conversations in Exercise 3.

■ THiNK SELF-ESTEEM ■
Being happy

1 Read these statements. Tick (✓) the ones that you think are important for being happy. Write a cross (✗) against the ones that you think are not so important.

1 There's no 'right' body shape or size. Healthy and happy people come in all shapes and sizes. ☐
2 You can only find out what kind of person someone is if you get to know them better. ☐
3 Never laugh about people for being too thin, too short, too tall or too fat. ☐
4 Never laugh at other people's jokes about people's looks. That's unfair and it hurts. ☐
5 Being thin is not the same as being healthy and happy. ☐
6 Like yourself for who you are and for the things you are good at. ☐

2 **SPEAKING** Work in pairs. Say what you think is important for being happy.

Pronunciation
Vowel sounds: /ɪ/ and /iː/
Go to page 120. 🔊

33

READING

1 Look at Jenny's blog for not more than 15 seconds and answer the questions. Then read and check your answers.

    1 How old is Jenny?

    2 How is she feeling?

    3 What's the problem?

2 Read the blog again. Answer the questions.

    1 How do Jenny's parents react to Jeremy's cooking?

    2 What does Jeremy sometimes do with the food his family don't eat?

    3 Why does Jeremy sing when he serves his spaghetti?

    4 What does Jenny like about the meals Jeremy serves?

    5 Why does Jenny say that her mum and dad's dance class is 'unhealthy'?

WRITING
Your favourite meal

1 Put the sentences or phrases in order to make an email from Jenny to her friend.

a		Actually this week it's not a surprise.
b		My brother always cooks a surprise meal for us then.
c		Best, Jenny
d		Would you like to come and try this week's surprise?
e		Are you free on Friday night?
f		It's pear and bean omelette.
g		Please say you can come.
h		And for dessert it's some ice cream and strawberries.
i	1	Dear Jimmy,
j		Doesn't that sound good?

2 Write out the email in your notebooks.

3 Write a paragraph describing your favourite or least favourite meal.

Thirteenandsosmart.com

HOME   ABOUT   NEWS   CONTACT

MY BLOG ABOUT MY DAY AND OTHER IMPORTANT THINGS

FRIDAY, 17TH MARCH

Not a good day. My older brother Jeremy is cooking tonight. 'What's the problem?' I can hear you saying. Well, the problem is that you don't know my brother. You don't know how he cooks. And you don't know that every Friday is a nightmare for me because my parents go to their dance class. When they come back we all sit down and Jeremy starts serving what he calls 'another surprise meal'. Jeremy isn't a bad cook. He's a catastrophe!

First of all he always cooks too many things, like fish, steak, boiled ham, roast chicken and sausages. All on one plate! That's too much food for a week! How can one person eat all that in one meal? Mum and Dad don't say a word, of course. They're too polite. And they don't want to give up their dance classes.

Spaghetti tonight. When Jeremy says 'spaghetti' he doesn't say it. He sings it (he loves cooking spaghetti, well, he loves cooking anything!). But that doesn't make a difference. It tastes terrible. There isn't enough tomato sauce on it. There's too much pasta. And there's too much salt. Yuck! Another one of my brother's favourites is vegetable soup. It's always too spicy, and there are never enough vegetables in it. And he puts in little pieces of fish, steak, ham, chicken and sausages. You can guess where they're from. It's the left-overs from the week before.

My brother's desserts aren't bad. He gets them at the supermarket. It's usually ice cream with strawberries or chocolate mousse with mango. But, of course, there are never enough strawberries and there's never enough ice cream. I want to talk to Mum and Dad today. I want them to give up dancing. It's not healthy. You know what I mean. It's unhealthy for me when they go dancing every Friday …

GRAMMAR
too many / too much / (not) enough + noun

1 **Complete the sentences with *much*, *many* and *enough* and then complete the rule.**

   1 He always cooks too _____ things.
   2 There's too _____ **salt** in the spaghetti.
   3 There's not _____ **tomato sauce** on it.
   4 There aren't _____ **vegetables** in the soup.
   5 There's not _____ **sugar** in my coffee.

   > RULE: Use *too* [1]_____ with countable nouns, and *too* [2]_____ with uncountable nouns.
   > Use *(not) enough* with [3]_____ and [4]_____ .

2 **Complete with *too much, too many, not enough*.**

   1 There are _____ mushrooms on this pizza. I hate them.
   2 There's _____ salt in this soup. I can't eat it.
   3 There is _____ sugar in my coffee. Can I have some more, please?
   4 There are _____ chairs. Can you stand?
   5 There are _____ cars on the road. It's dangerous to ride my bike.
   6 We've got _____ homework tonight. I want to watch TV.

too + adjective, (not +) adjective + enough

3 **Use the example sentences to ⟨circle⟩ the correct options in the rule.**

   *His vegetable soup is always **too spicy**.*
   *This pizza is **not hot enough**.*

   > RULE:
   > • We use *too* + adjective to say that something is [1]*more / less* than we like or want.
   > • We use *not* + adjective + *enough* to say that something is [2]*more / less* than we like or want.

4 **Complete the sentences.**

   0 The test is too easy. It's *not hard enough.*
   1 The film isn't exciting enough. It's _____
   2 The T-shirt is too expensive. It's _____
   3 It's not warm enough today. It's _____
   4 Your bike's too small for me. It's _____
   5 His car's not fast enough. It's _____

5 **Complete with *not enough* or *too*.**

My dad always says there's [1]_____ much rain in the UK in the summer, and that it's [2]_____ hot _____ . He's right. And I feel that it's [3]_____ boring to spend holidays here. So I'm happy that we usually go to the south of Italy for our holidays. There are kilometres of beaches, and so there are never [4]_____ many tourists. I love the food there, that's why I often eat [5]_____ much.

Workbook page 29 ⟶

VOCABULARY
Adjectives to talk about food

1 **Write the adjectives under the photos.**

   roast | boiled | grilled | fried

2 **Put the words in the list in order from 'very good' to 'very bad'.**

   nice | horrible | delicious | (a bit) boring

3 **SPEAKING** Work in pairs. Ask and answer questions. Use the words from Exercise 2.

   boiled or roast beef? | grilled or fried chicken? boiled or roast potatoes? | boiled or fried eggs? grilled or fried fish?

   > *What do you prefer, boiled or roast beef?*

   > *Roast beef. It's delicious.*

4 **How do you say these words in your language? Write two types of food next to each word.**

   sweet | spicy | savoury | fresh | tasty
   yummy | fatty | disgusting | salty

   sweet: chocolate, strawberries

Workbook page 30 ⟶

The picnic

1 🔊 1.38 **Look at the photos and discuss the questions. Then listen and read and check your answers.**

What food and drink have Megan and Luke got?
Why is Olivia unhappy?

MEGAN A picnic. I love picnics. What a great idea, Ryan.
OLIVIA Yes, Ryan. It was an awesome idea.
RYAN Don't be so surprised. It's not my first one.
LUKE Umm. Actually, I think it probably is.

OLIVIA What drinks have you got, Megan?
MEGAN Let me see. I've got orange juice, lemonade and apple juice. Oh, and some water as well.
OLIVIA That's great. What about you, Ryan?
RYAN I've got fruit: apples and bananas. Oh, and a couple of chocolate bars.

OLIVIA Luke? What about the sandwiches?
LUKE Well, I've got ham. I've got chicken, and tuna, and I've got a steak sandwich too.
OLIVIA That's all? But what about me? I can't eat that.
LUKE Why not?
OLIVIA Because I've got a problem with eating meat. I'm a vegetarian, remember?
LUKE So what? You can have the tuna sandwich, then.

RYAN Oh, Luke! Olivia is really upset now.
LUKE Is she upset with me? Why? Tell me. I've got no idea.
MEGAN She's a vegetarian, Luke. She doesn't eat meat. It's important to her.
LUKE Don't vegetarians eat fish?
MEGAN Maybe some do, but not Olivia.
LUKE Oh no!

DEVELOPING SPEAKING

2 Work in pairs. Discuss what happens next in the story. Write down your ideas.
We think Olivia eats a chicken sandwich.

3 ▶ EP2 Watch to find out how the story continues.

4 Mark the sentences T (True) or F (False).

1 Luke feels bad for not thinking about Olivia. ☐
2 Ryan has got lots of biscuits. ☐
3 Megan and Ryan play football against the other two. ☐
4 Luke secretly makes a phone call. ☐
5 They don't enjoy the football match. ☐
6 The pizza man brings Olivia a pizza with no meat on it. ☐

PHRASES FOR FLUENCY

1 Find the expressions 1–5 in the story. Who says them? Match them to the definitions a–f.

0 Actually, …   *Luke*   e
1 … as well.   ___   ☐
2 … a couple of …   ___   ☐
3 What about (me)?   ___   ☐
4 So what?   ___   ☐
5 upset with …   ___   ☐

a too
b unhappy with
c one or two (but not many)
d What is the situation (for me)?
e In fact, …
f Why is that a problem?

2 Complete the conversations. Use the expressions in Exercise 1.

1 A Mum? John's got his sandwiches. But _____ me?
  B Well, I'm making _____ cheese and tomato sandwiches for you right now.
  A Cool! Can I have an apple _____ ?
2 A I broke your watch. I'm sorry. Are you _____ me?
  B Don't worry about it. _____ , it wasn't a very good watch.
3 A I can't go to the cinema. I've got homework.
  B _____ ? You can do it at the weekend.

WordWise
Expressions with *have got*

1 Complete the things that Luke and Olivia say.

1 I've got a _____ with eating meat.
2 I've got _____ idea.
3 You go on. I've got _____ to do first.

2 Complete with the expressions in the list.

a problem | an idea | a headache | time | something to do

0 A Dad! I've got *a problem* with my English homework.
  B English? Sorry! I can't help you.
1 A Are you OK? Is something wrong?
  B I've got _____ . I want to go to bed.
2 A What can we do this afternoon?
  B I don't know.
  C Oh, I've got _____ !
3 A Jan, can you help me, please?
  B I'm really sorry, Tom. The lesson starts in two minutes! I haven't got _____ .
4 A Let's go to town tomorrow.
  B Tomorrow? Sorry, no, I've got _____ tomorrow. It's a secret!

Workbook page 30 ➤

FUNCTIONS
Apologising

1 Who says these sentences? Mark them O (Olivia) or L (Luke).

1 I'm really sorry. ___   3 Don't worry. ___
2 I feel bad. ___   4 It's OK. ___

2 🔊 1.39 Complete the conversation. Listen and check. Then act it out in pairs.

MAN   Oh no. I'm really [1] _____ .
WOMAN   [2] _____ worry. It's not my favourite picture.
MAN   But it's broken. I [3] _____ really bad.
WOMAN   [4] _____ OK. Really. I don't really like it anyway.

3 Work in pairs. Write a short dialogue for the picture below. Act it out.

READING

1 Find the pairs of words.

> daughter   brother   father
> wife   husband   mother
> son   sister

2 SPEAKING Describe each person in the picture. Use two words from Exercise 1.

> *The girl is a daughter and a sister.*

3 Work in pairs. Write down as many examples as you can of the following.

1 a TV brother and sister
2 a TV husband and wife

4 SPEAKING Compare your ideas with another pair.

5 🔊1.40 Read and listen to the article on page 39. Do they mention any of the families you talked about?

6 Read the article again. Correct the information in these sentences.

1 Bart Simpson has got a cat called Santa's Little Helper.
2 Lisa Simpson has got one aunt.
3 Ben Tennyson is on holiday in Europe.
4 He can change into 12 different aliens.
5 Greg Heffley has got a little brother called Roderick.
6 His ideas are always successful.

TV Families

Who is your favourite TV family? We want to know. It's not easy. There are so many great families to choose from. But to help you start thinking, here are some of ours.

Everyone knows *The Simpsons*; Bart, his mum and dad Marge and Homer, his sisters Lisa and Maggie. And then there's Granddad and those horrible aunts, Patty and Selma. And let's not forget Bart's dog, Santa's Little Helper. I love watching this family and their adventures around the town of Springfield. They get into all kinds of trouble but they never forget they are a family. And they always make me laugh. I love this show. Thanks, Dad, for introducing it to me.

When I was eight, *Ben 10* was my favourite TV programme. The story is crazy. Ten-year-old Ben Tennyson is spending his summer holiday with his Grandpa and his cousin Gwen. They are driving around the USA. One day Ben finds a strange watch and puts it on. Suddenly he is an alien. With this watch he can turn into ten different space creatures. But he needs these powers because some other evil alien wants Ben's new watch. So Ben spends the rest of the holiday fighting lots of monsters from outer space. But, of course, he still has time to fight with his cousin too.

The Heffley family are the stars of *Diary of a Wimpy Kid*, a really popular series of books and films centred around Greg, the middle son of the family. Greg lives with his mum and dad, his little brother Manny and his big brother Roderick. He's just a 'normal' kid who writes about his life in a journal. OK, so the Heffley family are not really a 'TV' family but they show the films on TV a lot so we think we can choose them. We want the Heffleys on our list because they are so funny. And we really love Greg and all the problems he has with his great ideas that never work out.

So these are three of our favourite TV families. Now write in and tell us about yours.

■ THiNK VALUES ■

TV families

1 Think about your favourite TV family. Tick (✓) the things they do.

My favourite TV family is _____ .

- They help each other.
- They fight a lot.
- They laugh a lot.
- They spend a lot of time together.
- They talk about their problems.
- They are good friends.

2 **SPEAKING** Work in pairs. Tell your partner about your favourite TV family. Are they a good family?

The Simpsons are usually a good family because ...

But sometimes they ...

GRAMMAR
Possessive adjectives and pronouns

1 **Complete the sentences with the words in the list. Look at the article on page 39 and check your answers.**

our | ours | your | yours

1 Who are _____ favourite TV family?
2 Here are some of _____ .
3 These are three of _____ favourite TV families.
4 Now write in and tell us about _____ .

2 **Complete the rule with *pronouns* and *adjectives*. Then complete the table.**

> **RULE:** Possessive ¹_____ come before a noun to show who something belongs to: *It's my book.*
>
> Possessive ²_____ can take the place of the possessive adjective and the noun: *The book is mine.*

possessive adjectives	possessive pronouns
0 It's __*my*__ book.	The book is __*mine*__
1 It's your book.	The book is _____ .
2 It's _____ book.	The book is hers.
3 It's _____ book.	The book is his.
4 It's our book.	The book is _____ .
5 It's _____ book.	The book is theirs.

whose and possessive 's

3 (Circle) **the correct words and complete the rule.**

A ¹*Whose / Who* son is Bart?
B Bart is ²*Homer's / Homers'* son.
A ³*Whose / Who's* Lisa's mum?
B Marge.

> **RULE:** To ask about possession, use the question word ¹_____ .
>
> To talk about possession, add ²_____ to the end of a name / noun.
>
> If the name / noun ends in an *-s*, add the apostrophe (') after the *-s*.

4 (Circle) **the correct words.**

1 A *Whose / Who* phone is this?
  B Ask Jenny. I think it's *her / hers*.
2 Hey! That's *my / mine* sandwich not *your / yours*.
3 I'm sure that's *Kate's / Kates'* bike. It looks just like *her / hers*.
4 A *Whose / Who* do you sit next to in Maths?
  B *Rashid / Rashid's*.
5 A Is that your *parent's / parents'* dog?
  B Yes, I think it's *their / theirs*.

> **Workbook page 36**

VOCABULARY
Family members

1 **Read the text. Complete the spaces in the picture with the missing family words.**

Here's a photo of my dad's side of the family. My dad's got a *big* brother called Bob. He's my *uncle* and he's great. He's so funny. His wife Jemma is my *aunt*, of course (and she's my dad's *sister-in-law*). She's also really nice. They've got two sons – Jimmy and his *little* brother Robin. They're my *cousins*. Jimmy is also my best friend.

Of course, my dad and Bob have the same mum and dad. They are my *grandparents*. I call them *Grandma Diana* and *Grandpa Roger*. They're really nice to me because I'm their only granddaughter.

2 **SPEAKING Work in pairs. How many sentences can you make about the family in two minutes?**

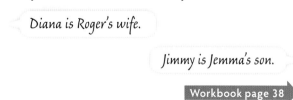

Diana is Roger's wife.

Jimmy is Jemma's son.

> **Workbook page 38**

my dad | ⁰ *Grandpa* Roger | ¹_____ Diana

Dad's ²_____ brother
My ³_____ Bob

Jimmy's ⁵_____ brother
Robin (my ⁶_____)

My ⁴_____ Jemma

My ⁷_____ Jimmy

LISTENING

1 **Read and match three of the sentences with the pictures. Write the numbers in the boxes.**

WHY MY FAMILY DRIVE ME MAD

1 My sister always wants to borrow my clothes. It drives me mad. (Lucy, 17)

2 My uncle tells really bad jokes. No one ever laughs – just him. (Howard, 15)

3 My dad never gives me any money. He's so mean. (Suzie, 16)

4 My grandpa just talks about the 'good-old days'. I'm not really interested. (Viv, 12)

5 I often fight with my parents about going out. They always want me to stay at home. (Tom, 14)

6 My brother plays games all day. He never lets me play. (Paul, 14)

2 ◄))1.41 **Listen to the conversations. What is the relationship between the speakers?**

Conversation 1: _____

Conversation 2: _____

3 ◄))1.41 **Listen again and answer the questions.**

1 What does Lucy's sister Kathy want to borrow?

2 Why does she want to borrow it?

3 Does Lucy say yes or no?

4 Where does Tom want to go?

5 What does his mum say?

6 What does his dad say?

Pronunciation

-er /ə/ at the end of words
Go to page 120. ◄))

FUNCTIONS
Asking for permission

1 **Complete the sentences from the listening.**

Asking for permission	Saying yes	Saying no
1 _____ I borrow your yellow and black shirt?	Of course you can.	No, you 3 _____ .
2 _____ I go out tonight?		

2 **Write a short conversation for the picture.**

3 **Think of requests that you make to different members of your family. Write them down.**

Can I borrow … ?   *Can I have … ?*

Can I go … ?   *Can I play … ?*

4 **Read them to your partner. Can he/she guess who you say this to?**

READING

1 Look at the photos. How do you think these girls were heroes? Read the article and find out.

THE SWIMMING POOL HEROES

Miya Peyregne, aged nine, and her six-year-old sister Tiffany were in the swimming pool in the back garden of their house in Grandville, Michigan, USA. Their father David was with them. It was a lovely day. There wasn't a cloud in the sky.

Suddenly David shouted. He was in trouble. It was his legs. His legs weren't right. He was in pain.

Then he was under the water. The girls weren't scared but they were worried. Was it just a joke or was he really in trouble? Twenty seconds later he was still under the water. Now Miya was scared.

There was no time to wait. In seconds Miya was under the water with her father. He was heavy but with the help of the water she was able to pull him to one side of the pool. Now his head was out of the water. He was alive but he wasn't conscious.

There was a mobile phone in the house. Tiffany called the emergency services. Ten minutes later an ambulance was there. Soon their father was conscious again. The girls were relieved.

David still doesn't know what was wrong with his legs on that day. But he knows that his daughters were heroes and thanks them every day for saving his life. He is a very proud father.

2 Read the article again. Put the sentences in the correct order. There is one thing not mentioned in the article. Where do you think it goes?

a Miya goes under the water to help her dad. ☐

b Tiffany phones for an ambulance. ☐

c Their mother arrives home. ☐

d David has a problem with his legs. ☐

e David disappears under the water. ☐

f Miya and Tiffany are swimming with their dad, David. ☐

■ TRAIN TO THiNK ■

Making inferences

1 Work in pairs. Who says these sentences? Mark them M (Miya), T (Tiffany) or D (Dad).

1 'Help. I'm in trouble.' ☐

2 'What's wrong, Dad?' ☐

3 'Help him. Go under the water.' ☐

4 'Call an ambulance.' ☐

5 'My dad needs help.' ☐

6 'My heroes.' ☐

2 Work in pairs. Write one more thing to say to each person.

1 Miya   4 The ambulance driver

2 Tiffany   5 The girls' mother

3 David

3 **SPEAKING** Read your sentences to another pair for them to guess.

I think Miya says that.

That's probably Tiffany.

GRAMMAR
was / were

1 **Look at the examples from the article on page 42. Circle the correct words.**

1 It *was / were* a lovely day. There *wasn't / weren't* a cloud in the sky.

2 The girls *were / weren't* scared but they *were / weren't* worried.

3 *Was / Were* he really in trouble?

2 **Complete the table.**

Positive	Negative
I/he/she/it [0] *was*	I/he/she/it [1] _____ (was not)
You/we/they [0] *were*	You/we/they [2] _____ (were not)

Questions	Short answers
[3] _____ I/he/she/it?	Yes, I/he/she/it [4] _____ . No, I/he/she/it [5] _____ .
[6] _____ you/we/they?	Yes, you/we/they [7] _____ . No, you/we/they [8] _____ .

3 **Complete the questions and answers with *was*, *were*, *wasn't* or *weren't*.**

1 A _____ you in bed at 9 pm last night?
  B No, I _____ . I _____ in the kitchen with my mum and dad.

2 A _____ your teacher happy with your homework?
  B Yes she _____ . She _____ very happy with it.

3 A _____ it hot yesterday?
  B No, it _____ . It _____ really cold.

4 A _____ we at school yesterday?
  B No, we _____ . It _____ Sunday!

5 A _____ your parents born in the UK?
  B No, they _____ . They _____ born in India.

4 **SPEAKING** Work in pairs. Ask and answer the questions in Exercise 3.

Workbook page 37

VOCABULARY
Feelings

1 **Match the sentences.**

1 Our daughter was first in the race. ☐
2 It was 9 pm and Mum wasn't home. ☐
3 That wasn't a nice thing to say to Miriam. ☐
4 That maths lesson was really difficult. ☐
5 I wasn't expecting a big party. ☐
6 The students were really noisy. ☐
7 It was a really good horror film. ☐
8 The test was really hard. ☐

a She's really **upset** now.
b And the teacher was **angry**.
c I was very **surprised** to see so many people there.
d I'm really **confused** now.
e We are so **proud** of her.
f I was **relieved** when it was over.
g I was a bit **worried**. Where was she?
h I was really **scared** at the end of it.

2 **Match the sentences in Exercise 1 with the pictures. Write the numbers 1–8.**

Workbook page 38

Culture

1 Look at the photos. What can you see? What's the same in the two photos?

2 🔊1.44 Read and listen to the article. Which countries do the photos show?

3 Do people celebrate Children's Day in your country? If so how do they celebrate it?

Around the world on Children's Day

In 1954 there was the first Universal Children's Day on 20th November to <u>celebrate</u> and protect children all over the world. This was <u>International</u> Children's Day but now many countries around the world have their own day each year when they celebrate their children.

1st June

BULGARIA: Parents do special things with their children and give them big **presents**. The day is like a second birthday for the children.

CHINA: This is a very special day in schools. They take the children on camping trips or trips to the cinema. Many children also get presents from their parents.

23rd April

TURKEY: This day is a **national** holiday in Turkey. On this day, Turkey invites groups of children from other countries to stay with Turkish families and celebrate with them.

24th July

VANUATU: Children spend the morning at school where they celebrate and have fun. At midday, the children are free to go home and spend the rest of the day with their parents. Some parents buy their children a present but the most important thing is for children and parents to have some time to spend **together**.

30th April

MEXICO: Children's day is called *El Día Del Niño*. Some schools close for the day, other schools have a special day for the children when they play games. The children also bring in their favourite food to **share** with their friends.

5th May

JAPAN: The official children's day, called *kodomo no hi*, is on 5th May. But some people in Japan celebrate two children's days. One on 3rd March for girls and one on 5th May for boys. On 5th May they fly carp streamers (a type of wind sock in the shape of a fish).

14th November

INDIA: Indians chose this day to celebrate because it is the birthday of the country's first Prime Minister, Jawaharlal Nehru. Nehru was famous for his love of children. On this day, the children organise the celebrations at their school. Their teachers sing and dance for the students.

4 Read the article again. Answer the questions. Sometimes there is more than one correct answer.

In which country …

1 do the children spend more time with their mum and dad?
2 do they have more than one Children's Day?
3 is Children's Day also a famous person's birthday?
4 do children get presents?
5 do children celebrate with children from other countries?
6 do children celebrate Children's Day at school?

5 SPEAKING Work in small groups. Talk about the perfect Children's Day.

All children get a big present. *School is closed for the whole day.*

Mum and Dad do your homework.

6 VOCABULARY There are six words in bold/underlined in the article. Match the words with these meanings. Write the words.

0 to have fun, do something special, for example on a friend's birthday — *celebrate*
1 with other people — _____
2 to do with a whole country — _____
3 to have something at the same time with other people — _____
4 to do with two or more countries — _____
5 something you give to a person on a special day — _____

WRITING
An invitation

1 Read the emails. Answer the questions.

1 Who is Dana?
2 Can Liam go to the party?

To: Liam_Walker@hooray.co.uk
Subject: Party!

Hi Liam,
Would you like to come to my house next Friday for a party at 7 pm? It's my cousin Dana's birthday.
My address is 32 Lime Street. Make a playlist please, I love your music.
Hope you can come. Let me know soon.
Tina
PS Don't tell Dana. It's a surprise.

To: TinaB@thinkmail.com
Subject: Re: Party!

Hi Tina,
I'd love to come to your party on Friday but I've got a small problem. I've got football training from 6 to 7.30 pm. Can I arrive a bit late? Is that OK?
No problem with the playlist. I've got some great new songs.
See you Friday.
Liam

---

2 Match the sentences with the same meaning. Write a–e in the boxes.

1 Would you like to come to my party? ☐
2 I'd love to come to your party. ☐
3 I'm sorry I can't come to your party. ☐
4 Make a playlist, please. ☐
5 Don't tell Dana. ☐

a I don't want Dana to know.
b Can you make a playlist?
c Can you come to my party?
d I'd love to come but I can't.
e I'd be very happy to accept your invitation.

3 Which pairs of sentences in Exercise 2 can you use to do these things?

1 give an order _____
2 accept an invitation _____
3 make a request _____
4 make an invitation _____
5 refuse an invitation _____

4 Read the invitation again. Answer the questions.

1 What is the invitation for?
2 What special requests does Tina make?

5 You want to invite a friend to your house. What information should you include? Tick (✓) the correct answers.

1 Your address. ☐
2 How many brothers and sisters you've got. ☐
3 The time you want them to come. ☐
4 The reason. ☐
5 Who your favourite singer is. ☐
6 The day or date you want them to come. ☐

6 Write an invitation (50 words). Choose one of these reasons. Include a special request or instruction.

- It's your birthday.
- You've got a great new DVD to watch.
- You've got a new computer game.

CAMBRIDGE ENGLISH: Key

■ THiNK EXAMS

READING AND WRITING
Part 2: Multiple-choice sentence completion   Workbook page 61 ▶

1   Read the sentences about a trip to a café. Choose the best word (A, B or C) for each space.

0	99% in my maths test! Mum is really _____ .	(A) proud	B scared	C upset
1	She takes me and my little _____ to the café for an ice cream.	A uncle	B aunt	C sister
2	I eat _____ of ice cream.	A many	B any	C a lot
3	My mum doesn't want her ice cream, so I eat _____ too.	A her	B mine	C hers
4	And then I drink _____ cola.	A not enough	B too many	C too much
5	I _____ feel very well, so we go home.	A not	B don't	C am not

Part 3: Dialogue matching   Workbook page 35 ▶

2   Complete the conversation. What does Anita say to the waiter?

    For questions 1–5, choose the correct letter A–H.

WAITER   Can I help you?

ANITA   (0) ___G___

WAITER   Of course, here you are.

(5 minutes later)

WAITER   OK, so what can I get you?

ANITA   (1) _____

WAITER   Of course. Would you like a starter?

ANITA   (2) _____

WAITER   And what would you like to drink?

ANITA   (3) _____

WAITER   And would you like a dessert?

ANITA   (4) _____

WAITER   OK, so that's a cheese omelette and strawberry ice cream.

(20 minutes later)

ANITA   (5) _____

WAITER   Of course. I'll be back soon.

A   How much is it?

B   An orange juice, please.

C   I'd like a cheese omelette, please.

D   And the orange juice.

E   Can I have the bill?

F   No, thanks. Just the omelette.

G   ~~I'd like to see the menu, please.~~

H   Yes, please. Can I have some strawberry ice cream?

LISTENING
Part 3: Three-option multiple-choice   Workbook page 43 ▶

3   ◀))1.45 Listen to Jackie talking to Oliver about her family. For each question, choose the right answer (A, B or C).

0	The party was last	(A) Friday evening.	B Saturday evening.	C Friday afternoon.
1	The party was for Oliver's	A brother.	B dad.	C uncle.
2	Oliver's uncle is	A 20.	B 34.	C 44.
3	Oliver's aunt is called	A Anna.	B Carla.	C Ruth.
4	Mike is Oliver's	A brother.	B dad.	C cousin.
5	Oliver has got	A two sisters.	B one sister.	C one sister and one brother.

TEST YOURSELF

VOCABULARY

1 **Complete the sentences with the words in the list. There are two extra words.**

angry | big | boiled | grilled | relieved | scared
grandparents | carrots | confused | spicy | chicken | proud

1 I don't like many vegetables – just peppers and _____ .
2 I was really worried about the exam so I was _____ when it was over.
3 The curry is too _____ . I can't eat it.
4 It was a really stupid thing to do. My parents were really _____ with me.
5 To make _____ potatoes you need to cook them in water for about 20 minutes.
6 There was a strange noise outside the house. We were a bit _____ .
7 Nigel's a vegetarian. He doesn't eat _____ .
8 I don't really understand this homework. I'm a bit _____ .
9 Freddie's my _____ brother. I'm 14 and he's 20.
10 My mum's mother and father are my _____ .

/10

GRAMMAR

2 **Complete the sentences with the words in the list.**

much | many | ours | our | was | were

1 How _____ sugar do you want in your coffee?
2 It _____ really cold yesterday.
3 That's not your dog, it's _____ .
4 There are too _____ socks on your bedroom floor!
5 _____ dog's called Spike.
6 Where _____ you last night?

3 **Find and correct the mistake in each sentence.**

1 This salad has got too much beans.
2 That's not your sandwich. It's my.
3 My parents was very proud of my school report.
4 I like Clara and I really like hers sister too.
5 How many water do you want?
6 I think this is Kevins' book.

/12

FUNCTIONAL LANGUAGE

4 **Write the missing words.**

1 A I'm late. I'm really _____ .
  B Don't _____ . We've still got lots of time.
2 A I _____ this question is really difficult.
  B I think _____ too.
3 A _____ I borrow your bike, Dad?
  B Of _____ you can.
4 A Can I go _____ tonight?
  B No, you _____ .

/8

MY SCORE _____ /30

| 22 – 30 |
| 10 – 21 |
| 0 – 9 |

5 IT FEELS LIKE HOME

OBJECTIVES

FUNCTIONS: making suggestions; talking about events in the past

GRAMMAR: past simple (regular verbs); modifiers: *quite*, *very*, *really*

VOCABULARY: parts of a house and furniture; adjectives with *-ed* / *-ing*; phrasal verbs with *look*

 A

 B

 C

 D

 E

 F

READING

1 🔊1.46 Match the words in the list with the photos. Write 1–6 in the boxes. Then listen, check and repeat.

1 kitchen | 2 bedroom | 3 bathroom
4 living room | 5 dining room | 6 garden

2 Match the verbs in the list with the rooms in Exercise 1. (Some verbs go with more than one room.)

eat | sleep | cook | wash
watch TV | play football

3 SPEAKING Work in pairs. Have you got the same ideas? What other activities do you do in these rooms?

> I talk to my dad in the kitchen.

> I sing in the bathroom.

4 SPEAKING Look at the photos on page 49. What can you say about the house?

5 🔊1.47 Read and listen to the magazine article. Choose the correct option A, B or C.

1 The queue of people wanted to help James May to buy a house.
  A Right B Wrong C Doesn't say

2 They finished building the house in one month.
  A Right B Wrong C Doesn't say

3 The LEGO fridge worked.
  A Right B Wrong C Doesn't say

4 James May liked the bed.
  A Right B Wrong C Doesn't say

5 There were photos of the house on a Facebook page.
  A Right B Wrong C Doesn't say

6 A charity for children has got the pieces of LEGO now.
  A Right B Wrong C Doesn't say

The LEGO® House

A few years ago in August, there was a very long queue of people in the countryside near London, in England. Some people started queuing at 4.30 in the morning. Why were they there? They wanted to help James May, a TV presenter, to build a house. But this was not an ordinary house. No, this was a LEGO house.

Together, 1,200 people used 3.3 million (yes, 3,300,000) LEGO toy bricks to make a real house.

It was part of a TV show called *Toy Stories*. In the programmes, James May used traditional toys to make 'real' things. Why LEGO? Well, because when he was young, James May loved LEGO and played with it all the time.

The people finished building the house on 17 September, almost seven weeks after they started. Everything was LEGO. All the walls, doors and windows were LEGO. There was a LEGO bedroom and a LEGO bed. There was a LEGO bathroom with a LEGO toilet and a shower – and they worked! In the kitchen there was a LEGO fridge (but no cooker) and there were LEGO tables and chairs. There was even a LEGO cat. James May stayed in the house one night and was surprised because the bed was quite comfortable.

At first, a theme park called LEGOLAND planned to buy the house, but later they decided not to. James May tried to find another buyer. He started a Facebook page and asked other people to buy it, but nobody wanted it. So on 22 September, they started to take the house to pieces. A few days later, there wasn't a LEGO house any more.

James May was not happy about it as more than 1,000 people worked hard to build the house and everything inside it. Other people were not so sad. The television company donated the three million LEGO pieces to a charity for children.

THiNK VALUES

Community spirit

1 Read what people said about the LEGO house. Match the activities a–d with the comments 1–4.

a working together   c having fun
b being creative   d caring for others

1 *We really enjoyed this – we laughed a lot.* ☐

2 *The idea of building a LEGO cat was really interesting.* ☐

3 *I loved being with so many people, doing the same thing!* ☐

4 *I think it's great that they donated the LEGO pieces to a charity for children.* ☐

2 **SPEAKING** Put the activities a–d in Exercise 1 in order of importance for you. Compare your ideas with a partner.

I think working together is really important. It's my number 1.

Me too. It's my number 2.

What's your number 1?

Caring for others.

GRAMMAR
Past simple (regular verbs)

1 Find the past simple forms of these verbs in the article and write them below. Then complete the rules.

0	start	*started*	5	stay	_____
1	want	_____	6	plan	_____
2	use	_____	7	decide	_____
3	finish	_____	8	try	_____
4	work	_____	9	ask	_____

> **RULE:** Use the past simple to talk about finished actions in the past.
>
> **With regular verbs:**
> * We usually add [1]_____ to the verb (e.g. *start – started / stay – stayed*).
> * If the verb ends in -e (e.g. *use*), we add [2]_____ .
> * If a short verb ends in consonant + vowel + consonant (e.g. *plan*), we double the [3]_____ and add *-ed*.
> * We add *-ed* to verbs ending in vowel + *-y* (e.g. *stayed*).
> * If the verb ends in consonant + *-y* (e.g. *try*), we change the *-y* to [4]_____ and add [5]_____ .

2 Complete the sentences. Use the past simple form of the verbs.

0 When my granddad was young, he *played* (play) with LEGO all the time.

1 We _____ (start) to paint our house last month, and we _____ (finish) yesterday.

2 She _____ (decide) to change her bedroom, so she _____ (paint) the walls pink.

3 We _____ (try) to find another house last year because we _____ (want) to move.

4 I _____ (visit) my aunt and uncle because they _____ (want) to show me their new flat.

5 My parents _____ (study) lots of ideas for a new kitchen before they _____ (order) it.

6 On my last holiday, I _____ (stay) with my grandparents and _____ (help) them tidy up the garden.

7 Last weekend Jack _____ (plan) to organise his room but he _____ (watch) television instead.

Workbook page 46

Pronunciation
-ed endings /d/, /t/, /ɪd/
Go to page 120.

VOCABULARY
Furniture

1 🔊1.50 Match the words with the photos. Write 1–12 in the boxes. Then listen, check and repeat.

1 armchair | 2 carpet | 3 cooker | 4 curtains
5 desk | 6 lamp | 7 mirror | 8 shelves
9 shower | 10 sofa | 11 toilet | 12 wardrobe

2 **SPEAKING** Work in pairs. Where are these things in your house? Tell your partner.

> *There are mirrors in our bathroom, in my parents' bedroom and in our living room.*

Workbook page 48

LISTENING

1 SPEAKING Work in pairs. Describe the pictures.

2 🔊 1.51 Listen to four people talking about 'home'. Write the names under the correct pictures.

Sophie | James | Mia | Daniel

3 🔊 1.51 Listen again. Complete the table with the missing information.

	What is home?	What I like doing there.
Sophie	Home is where I feel ¹_____ .	²_____
James	Somewhere ³_____ .	⁴_____
Mia	The ⁵_____ in our flat.	⁶_____
Daniel	With ⁷_____ in the garden.	⁸_____

GRAMMAR
Modifiers: *quite, very, really*

1 Write the name of the person from Exercise 3 who says these things. Then underline the words before the adjectives and complete the rule.

1 I feel really happy there. _____
2 Our kitchen is quite small. _____
3 The armchair is very comfortable. _____

> **RULE:** Use words *very*, *really* and *quite* to say more about an adjective.
>
> The words *very* and ¹_____ are used to make an adjective stronger. The word ²_____ usually means 'a little bit'.

2 Write true sentences about your home using the words.

0 kitchen – big / small
  Our kitchen isn't very big / It's quite small.
1 bedroom – tidy / untidy
2 sofa – comfortable / uncomfortable
3 home – busy / quiet ▸ Workbook page 47

■ THiNK SELF-ESTEEM ■
Feeling safe

1 Think about the questions and make notes.

1 Where do you feel 'at home'? Describe the place.
2 What's most important for you there? (furniture? things? colours? people?)
3 What does that place feel like for you? (relaxing? safe? comfortable?)

2 SPEAKING Write 2 or 3 sentences about where you feel at home. Read them out in groups.

> I feel at home in my bedroom. My bed is quite small but it's very comfortable. I like lying on it and thinking about my life.

> I feel at home when I'm with my family. My mum and dad are great and my brother is my best friend. I love doing things with them.

> I feel at home in the living room. Our sofa is really comfortable. I love sitting there on my own reading a good book.

READING

1 Read Jenny's holiday blog and complete the sentences with a word or a number.

DAY 5

Dad gets it right! (finally)

Day five of the Italian adventure and we're in Naples. We arrived here early yesterday morning, but as usual we were only at the hotel for about five minutes before Dad wanted to take us somewhere. This time it was to the ancient city of Pompeii near Naples. I didn't really want to go. I wanted to go shopping for shoes.

We travelled there by train. The journey didn't take long – but long enough for Dad to tell us a bit about the history. Many years ago, Pompeii was a large Italian city near a volcano called Mount Vesuvius – then on 24 August 79 CE – the volcano erupted and completely covered the city in ash. It killed about 20,000 people. But the ash didn't destroy the buildings and now, 2,000 years later, you can walk around the city and see how people lived all those years ago.

2,000-year-old houses: thanks, Dad – really boring, I thought, but I was wrong! The houses were very interesting. Most of them were really big with lots of rooms (so lots of space to get away from annoying brothers and sisters!) There were paintings and mosaics all over the walls. I'd love a Roman mosaic of One Direction on my bedroom wall. Also, I was amazed at the bathrooms. I'd love a big bathroom in our house – ours is so small!

I got really interested in Pompeii. I wasn't bored at all. In fact, I've got lots of ideas for our house when we get home!

Mount Vesuvius – a real ¹_____ . (I hope it doesn't erupt!)

More than ²_____ people died here, all of them covered in ash.

The paintings and ³_____ are really beautiful.

The houses in this ancient city are more than ⁴_____ years old.

---

2 Answer the questions.

1 Where is Jenny's family staying at the moment?
2 How did they go to Pompeii?
3 What did Jenny's dad tell them about on the way there?
4 When did Vesuvius erupt?
5 What did Jenny like about the Pompeii houses?
6 What was Jenny's overall opinion of Pompeii?

WRITING

Use your answers in Exercise 2 to write a summary of the text in no more than 100 words.

Jenny didn't want to go to Pompeii and ...

GRAMMAR
Past simple negative

1 **Compete the sentences from Jenny's blog and then complete the rule.**

1 I _____ really want to go.

2 The journey _____ take long.

3 The ash _____ destroy the buildings.

> **RULE:** To make any verb negative in the past simple, use _____ + the base form of the verb.

2 **Here are some more things Jenny wrote about Pompeii. Make them negative.**

0 We visited all of the houses.
We didn't visit all of the houses.

1 I wanted to go home.

2 The poor people lived in big houses.

3 Dad ordered a pizza for lunch.

4 It rained in the afternoon.

3 **SPEAKING** **Work in pairs. Tell your partner two things that you did and two things that you didn't do last weekend. Choose from the verbs in the list.**

work | climb | play | travel | clean
help | study | use | dance | walk

I didn't watch any TV.　　*I visited my friends.*

> Workbook page 47

VOCABULARY
adjectives with *-ed* / *-ing*

1 **How is Jenny feeling? Write the adjectives under the pictures.**

annoyed | relaxed | bored | interested | amazed

> **LOOK!** We use *-ed* adjectives to say how we feel about something.
> We use *-ing* adjectives to say what we think about something or to describe something.

2 **What did Jenny say about Pompeii? Complete the sentences with *interested* or *interesting*.**

1 I got really _____ in Pompeii.

2 The houses were very _____ .

3 (Circle) **the correct words.**

1 I get *annoyed / annoying* when people ignore me.

2 His painting was brilliant. I was *amazed / amazing*.

3 Bob talks about football all the time! He's really *bored / boring*.

4 A hot shower is always very *relaxed / relaxing*.

5 I think Maths is really *interested / interesting*.

4 **Complete the sentences so that they are true for you.**

1 I'm never bored when _____ .

2 I find _____ really annoying.

3 _____ is the most amazing singer.

4 I'm really interested in _____ .

5 I'm never relaxed when _____ .

5 **SPEAKING** **Work in pairs. Compare your answers.**

> Workbook page 48

WRITING
A blog post

1 **Think about a real holiday that you went on or an invented holiday. Make notes about these questions.**

1 Where did you go?

2 Who did you go with?

3 What did you do that was very special / different?

4 What did you like / not like about the holiday?

5 What was *boring / exciting / amazing / interesting / annoying* about the holiday?

2 **Use your notes from Exercise 1 to write a blog post about your holiday. Write about 120–150 words. Write three paragraphs.**

Paragraph 1 – your answers to 1 and 2

Paragraph 2 – your answer to 3

Paragraph 3 – your answers to 4 and 5

1 _____　　2 _____

3 _____

4 _____

5 _____

Hey, look at that guy!

1 **Look at the photos and answer the questions.**

What do you think the four friends are saying about the man? What do they know about him?

2 🔊 1.52 **Now read and listen to the photostory. Check your answers.**

1

RYAN Stop looking at your satnav – we know how to get to school.
OLIVIA Very funny. Hey, look at that guy!
RYAN What about him?
MEGAN I think he was here yesterday too.

2

LUKE So? A homeless guy. It's not a big deal.
RYAN That's right.
OLIVIA He's got problems. Don't you care?
RYAN Well, to be honest – no, not very much.

3

MEGAN But it's really sad!
OLIVIA I know what you mean. I watched a programme on TV a while ago about homeless people. Awful!
MEGAN Can you imagine? No place to live. It must be horrible.
LUKE Well, I'm sure that's true. But it's not really our problem.

4

OLIVIA Let's go and talk to him.
RYAN Hang on! Do you think that's a good idea?
MEGAN What do you mean? He's poor, but that doesn't mean he's dangerous.
LUKE OK, maybe not dangerous. He's probably not very nice, though.
OLIVIA Maybe he needs help.

DEVELOPING SPEAKING

3 Work in pairs. Discuss what happens next in the story. Write down your ideas.

We think the boys go to school but Megan and Olivia talk to the man.

4 ◄ EP3 Watch to find out how the story continues.

5 Put the sentences in the correct order. Write 1–8 in the boxes.

- [ ] a The students decide to ask somebody from a charity for help.
- [ ] b The girls are worried about the man.
- [ ] c When they go back to the park, the man gives Olivia her necklace.
- [1] d The friends are on their way to school.
- [ ] e Other students start laughing at her.
- [ ] f Ryan tells the other students about the homeless person.
- [ ] g In the park, they see a homeless person.
- [ ] h The teacher notices that Olivia is not paying attention.

PHRASES FOR FLUENCY

1 Find these expressions in the story. Who says them?

1 … not a big deal. _____
2 …, to be honest, … _____
3 I know what you mean. _____
4 it's not really our problem. _____
5 Hang on! _____
6 …, though. _____

2 Use the expressions in Exercise 1 to complete the dialogues.

1 A She's usually a nice girl. She sometimes gets a bit angry, _____ .
  B _____ . Yesterday she really shouted at me!
2 A I need help. You've got to help me with my homework!
  B _____ ! It's *your* homework – so really, _____ .
3 A It's only a small test tomorrow. Ten questions. It's _____ . Right?
  B Well, _____ , I'm a bit worried about it.

WordWise
Phrasal verbs with *look*

1 Look at these sentences from the story. Complete them with the words from the list.

after | up | for | at | into

1 Hey, look _____ that guy!
2 The charity looks _____ homeless people.
3 I'm just looking it _____ on my phone.
4 We need to look _____ why he's homeless.
5 Let's look _____ him.

2 (Circle) the correct word in each dialogue.

1 A What's Janet doing?
  B She's looking *after / like* the baby.
2 A Why are you looking *for / at* me like that?
  B Because I'm angry with you.
3 A I can't find my pen.
  B I'll help you look *after / for* it.
4 A Do the police know what happened?
  B No, they are still looking *for / into* it.
5 A What does this word mean?
  B I don't know. Let's look it *after / up* in the dictionary.

➤ Workbook page 48

FUNCTIONS
Making suggestions

1 Complete the sentences from the story with words from the lists. Then write ✓ (agree), ✗ (disagree) or ? (uncertain).

A How | could | Let's | Why
B idea | do | great | sure

0 A ___How___ about asking our parents for money?
  B I don't think that's a good ___idea___ . ✗
1 A _____ don't we try and help him?
  B I'm not so _____ . _____
2 A _____ give him our school lunch.
  B Let's _____ that. _____
3 A We _____ take him a bit of food after school.
  B I think that's a _____ idea. _____

ROLE PLAY At a market

2 Work in pairs. Student A: Go to page 127. Student B: Go to page 128. Take two or three minutes to prepare. Then have a conversation.

OBJECTIVES

FUNCTIONS: talking about past events; saying what you like doing alone and with others; talking about friends and friendships

GRAMMAR: past simple (irregular verbs); double genitive; past simple questions

VOCABULARY: past time expressions; personality adjectives

1

2

3

4

READING

1 **SPEAKING** Look at the photos. Say what the people are doing.

> *They're surfing the Internet.*

2 **SPEAKING** Match these words with the photos and compare with a partner. (Some words go with more than one photo.)

alone | together | happy
sad | bored | excited

> *In photo 1 they're together and they're excited.*

3 **SPEAKING** Work in pairs. Talk about things you like doing alone and other things you like doing together with other people. Here are some ideas to help you.

watch a film | walk
do homework | study | read
have breakfast | go shopping

> *I like going shopping with friends. I don't like going alone! I like doing homework alone.*

4 Look at the photos on page 57. What kind of television show is this? Who are the boy and the girl?

5 🔊 1.53 Read and listen to the web article. Check your ideas.

6 Read the article again. Correct the information in these sentences.

1 Their parents had the idea of them singing together.
2 Jonathan thought that Charlotte didn't look right for the show.
3 Charlotte and Jonathan were the same age.
4 Everyone laughed when Charlotte and Jonathan came out.
5 Simon Cowell said that Jonathan needed to sing with another girl.
6 Jonathan told Simon Cowell that he wanted to go home.
7 Jonathan and Charlotte came first in the competition.
8 They recorded a song called *Together*.

Together ⭐

In a school in England, a few years ago, a teenage girl heard a boy singing in another room. She liked it, and found out that the boy's name was Jonathan Antoine. The girl – Charlotte Jaconelli – also liked singing. A little later, the music teacher at school suggested that they could sing together. They did, and they started singing together as a duo. They also became very good friends. They even sang together at the music teacher's wedding.

Around that time, there was a television programme called *Britain's Got Talent* – a show to find new singers and performers. Charlotte wanted to enter the show with Jonathan but he was worried about the way he looked. However, Charlotte persuaded him and they went on the show. Charlotte was 16 and Jonathan was 17.

They did the first audition in April 2012. When they came onto the stage, they were very nervous. The four judges didn't think they looked good. Some people in the audience laughed when they saw them. Then they began to sing and everyone was amazed. They sang incredibly well – especially Jonathan. When they finished, people stood up and clapped.

All the judges thought Charlotte and Jonathan were great, but one judge, Simon Cowell, suggested that Jonathan sing on his own without Charlotte because, although she was good, he was fantastic.

Jonathan didn't think for long. He looked at his friend, and then looked back at the judges, and said that he wanted to stay in the competition with Charlotte. They carried on together, but they didn't win the competition – they came second. (A dancing dog won!) However, they weren't disappointed.

A few weeks later, Simon Cowell gave them the chance to record a CD. They made the CD, and then they thought about a title for it. They chose the word: 'Together'.

■ THiNK VALUES ■

Friendship and loyalty

1 **Choose the best way to finish this sentence.**

I think this story tells us that, in life, it is important …

1 … to look good.
2 … to be good at what you do.
3 … to come first.
4 … to look after your friends.
5 … to be nice to other people.
6 … to have lots and lots of friends.

2 SPEAKING **Compare your ideas with a partner.**

3 SPEAKING **Choose three of the values in Exercise 1. Put them in order of importance for you (1, 2, 3). Then compare with others.**

> *I think the most important thing is to look after your friends.*

> *That's my number 3. I think it's really important to be nice to other people.*

GRAMMAR

Past simple (irregular verbs)

1   Read these sentences about the article on page 57. All the verbs are in the past simple. How are the verbs in 1 different from the verbs in 2?

   1 She **liked** singing.
      They **started** as a duo.
      Some people **laughed**.

   2 They **sang** together.
      People **stood** up.
      We **came** here as a duo.

2   Look back at the article on page 57. Write the past simple forms of these verbs.

   0 find   _found_   4 think _____
   1 become _____   5 come _____
   2 go   _____   6 give   _____
   3 see   _____   7 make _____

3   Find at least four more irregular past simple forms in the article on page 57. Write the verbs.

4   Correct these two sentences from the article. Make them negative.

   1 Jonathan thought for a long time.
   2 They won the competition.

5   Look at the pictures and the prompts and write the sentences in the past simple.

Workbook page 54

VOCABULARY

Past time expressions

1   Complete the lists with appropriate expressions.

When we talk about the past, we often use expressions like these:

- yesterday, yesterday [1]_____ , yesterday afternoon
- last night, last week, last [2]_____ , last December
- an hour ago, two weeks ago, a month ago, [3]_____ ago

2   Complete the sentences with a time expression with *ago*.

   0 Andy is twenty. He left school when he was sixteen.
      Andy left school four years ago.
   1 It's 8 o'clock. I had breakfast at 7 o'clock.
      I had breakfast _____
   2 It's 10.20. The film began at 10.00.
      The film _____
   3 It's December. Your holiday was in July.
      My holiday _____

3   Complete the sentences with your own information. Use irregular verbs.

   1 A year ago, I _____ .
   2 Ten years ago, I _____ .
   3 Last year, I _____ .
   4 Yesterday morning, I _____ .
   5 Last night, I _____ .

Workbook page 56

1   We / go / to Italy but we / go / to Rome.
   We went to Italy but we didn't
   go to Rome.

2   I / see / Mark but I / see / Alicia.
   _____
   _____

3   Sue / come / to my party / but Dan / come.
   _____
   _____

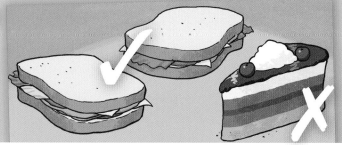

4   I make / sandwiches but I / make / cake.
   _____
   _____

LISTENING

1 **Which sentences do you agree with?**

1 Footballers are never friends with players from other teams.
2 Footballers never help other players.
3 Footballers only want to win cups.

2 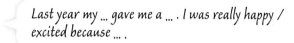 **Listen to a story about Cristiano Ronaldo. Tick (✓) the correct box.**

The two friends think the story is …

☐ certainly true.
☐ possibly true.
☐ certainly not true.

3 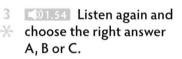 **Listen again and choose the right answer A, B or C.**

1 What was the family name of Ronaldo's friend?
  A Albert
  B The boy doesn't remember.
  C The boy didn't find the name.
2 How many places were there at the football school?
  A one   B two   C three
3 Why did Albert pass the ball to Cristiano?
  A Because Albert wanted a friend.
  B Because Albert was tired.
  C Because Cristiano was a better player.
4 What was the final score of the game?
  A 1–1   B 2–0   C 3–0
5 What is Albert's job now?
  A He's a footballer.
  B We don't know.
  C He drives cars.
6 What did Ronaldo give to his friend?
  A A car.
  B A house.
  C A car and a house.

4 **SPEAKING** Work in pairs. Tell your partner about a great present someone gave you.

Last year my ... gave me a ... . I was really happy / excited because ... .

GRAMMAR
Double genitive

1 **Read the sentence. Then choose the correct options to complete the rule.**

Ronaldo was there, and there was a friend of his called Albert.

> **RULE:** We form the 'double genitive' with noun + *of* + possessive [1]*pronoun / adjective* (mine, yours, his, hers, ours, yours, theirs).
> We also form the 'double genitive' with noun + *of* + possessive adjective (my, your, his, her, our, your, their) + noun + possessive *'s*.
> We use it to talk about [2]*one of many things / many things that we have.*

2 **Circle** the correct words.

0 She's a friend of me / mine.
1 Mr Smith is a teacher of my sister / my sister's.
2 She's a cousin of John / John's.
3 Mrs Jones is a neighbour of ours / us.

3 **Rewrite the underlined parts of the sentences.**

0 See that man? He's my father's friend.
  He's *a friend of my father's* .
1 Steve is our friend.
  Steve is _____ .
2 Mike borrowed my shirt.
  Mike borrowed _____ .
3 I lost my mum's book.
  I lost _____ .

> Workbook page 55 ➤

TRAIN TO THiNK

Making decisions

1 **Draw a mind map.**
• Complete the three circles with names of people who are close to you (friends, family).
• What do these people like? Write your ideas on the lines.

2 **SPEAKING** Work in groups. Imagine it's their birthdays. Show your mind maps, make suggestions and decide on a present for each person.

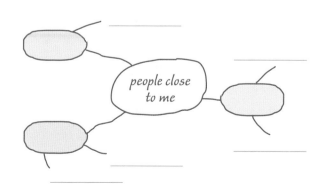

people close to me

READING

1 Read the magazine article quickly. Complete the sentences.

1 Richard and Sharon met for the first time on

_____ .

2 The second time they met, they went

_____ .

2 Read the article again. Put the events in the order they happened. Write the numbers 1–8.

☐	**a** Richard and Sharon go to a show together.
☐	**b** Richard has an accident.
☐	**c** Richard gives Sharon a present.
☐	**d** Sharon saves Richard's life.
☐	**e** Richard goes to hospital.
☐	**f** Sharon calls Richard.
1	**g** Richard goes surfing.
☐	**h** Richard sees Sharon for the first time.

3 **SPEAKING** Work in pairs. Tell the story. Use the ideas in Exercise 2. Put them into the past simple tense.

Richard went surfing. He had an accident ...

FUNCTIONS
Talking about past events

1 Think about a time when you made a new friend. Make notes.

- Who?
- When?
- Where?
- What happened?

2 In pairs tell your story.

I met my friend Al five years ago. I was on holiday in France with my family. We were in a small hotel. Al's family were in the same hotel. We made friends on the first day and spent all the holiday together.

How we met

This week lifeguard Sharon Evans and student Richard Lambert tell our reporter about their friendship and how they almost never met.

So first of all, when and where did you meet?

Richard We first met in 2012, one morning at about 10.30 am on Bondi Beach, in Sydney.

Sharon Actually, we met in the water.

OK, so how did you meet?

Richard I was out in the deep water on my surfboard when another board knocked me on the head. The next thing I knew, I was on the beach looking up at this face.

Sharon I was on the beach that day. I saw what happened so I swam out and brought Richard back in. He was unconscious, but luckily I got him to start breathing again. But for a minute I thought he was dead.

Richard And then they took me to hospital. I didn't have a chance to even say thanks to Sharon.

So what did you do?

Richard There was a really big show the next week with a popular Belgian-Australian singer called Gotye. I bought two tickets for Sharon and left them at work for her a few days later. I thought she could take someone with her. I also left her a note to say thanks with my telephone number on it.

Sharon He was really generous. They were expensive tickets.

Did you take a friend to the show?

Sharon I didn't know who to take and then I had a great idea.

What was it?

Richard Well, when I got home from work that day there was a voicemail on my phone. It was Sharon. She invited me to go with her. We had a great time. She was so cheerful and easy-going. We became really good friends right away.

GRAMMAR
Past simple questions

1 Put the words in order to make questions. Check your answers in the article on page 60.

    1 do / did / what / you / ?   2 did / you / meet / how / ?   3 friend / show / take / you / a / to / did / the / ?

2 Complete the table.

Question	Answer
¹_____ I/you/he/she/we/they enjoy the show?	Yes, I/you/he/she/we/they ³_____ . No, I/you/he/she/we/they ⁴_____ (did not).
What time ²_____ I/you/he/she/we/they get home?	I/you/he/she/we/they ⁵_____ home at midnight.

3 Match the questions and answers.

    1 Did you have a good weekend?   a Yes, I did. I completed four levels.
    2 Did you play computer games yesterday?   b We met at school four years ago.
    3 Where did you meet your best friend?   c We had chicken and chips.
    4 Who did you text yesterday?   d No, I didn't. It rained all the time.
    5 What did you have for dinner last night?   e I texted my best friend.

4 **SPEAKING** Work in pairs. Ask the questions 1–5 and give your own answers.   Workbook page 55

VOCABULARY
Personality adjectives

Look at the pictures. Read the sentences and write the names under the people.

Thank you.

It's OK. Don't worry.

1 _____
2 _____
3 _____
4 _____
5 _____
6 _____
7 _____
8 _____

MY FRIENDS

- Nick is intelligent. He knows a lot about everything
- Amelia is cheerful. She's always got a smile on her face.
- Kai is jealous. He's not happy when you talk to other friends.
- Ben is helpful. He's always ready to help you.
- Ruby is confident. She's not scared to talk in public.
- Liz is generous. She's always happy to share her things with you.
- Chloe is easy-going. She never gets angry about anything.
- Connor is funny. He always makes me laugh.

Pronunciation
Stressed syllables in words
Go to page 120.

Workbook page 56

Culture

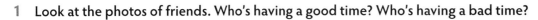

1 Look at the photos of friends. Who's having a good time? Who's having a bad time?

2 ◀)) 1.57 Read and listen to the web page. Five people commented on the different myths about friendship. Match the people to the myths.

Myth 1 _____ Myth 2 _____ Myth 3 _____ Myth 4 _____ Myth 5 _____

3 **SPEAKING** Which of the five people here do you agree with? Who do you disagree with? Compare with others in the class.

Friendship **myths**

Everyone wants to have friends, and **friendships** are important to teenagers all over the world. However, when people start a friendship, they sometimes expect too much from it. Here are five things about friendship that some people believe are true. But in fact they aren't – they are myths.

Myth no. 1: Friends are there to make you happy.

Myth no. 2: A real friend will never disappoint you.

Myth no. 3: The more friends you have, the better.

Myth no. 4: Friends share everything.

Myth no. 5: If you've got no friends, something's wrong with you.

We spoke to teens from different countries. Read what they think.

Burcu, Istanbul, Turkey
Nobody's perfect, so why do we think friends can be perfect? We all make mistakes, so it's only normal that there are times when good friends make mistakes, too. Perhaps you think that a really good friend always knows what you need. That's wrong – be careful! Sometimes you need to say to your friends, 'Please do this' or 'Don't do that'. Don't forget that there are times when your friends are **stressed** or unhappy, too. Then they can't help you the way you would like them to. **1**

Flávia, São Paulo, Brazil
There can be times in your life when you've got a lot of friends, and other times when you've only got one or two. Maybe you haven't got any friends **right now** because, for example, you're in a new city or school. When you haven't got any friends, it's important to wait and **be patient**. Make sure you're a friendly person – so other people want to **make friends** with you! **2**

Fernanda, Quito, Ecuador
You want to be a good friend, right? To build a good friendship, it's important to have fun together, to listen to your friends when they've got a problem, to help them when they need you, or just to go and watch a film together, or play some sport. And that takes time! That's why I think it's better to have one or two friends, and not a lot of friends. **4**

Luca, Florence, Italy
No, they don't! It takes time to build a good friendship. You don't want to tell your friend everything about yourself on the first day of your friendship. You and your friends want to share some things. But it's important to **remember** that there are other things that you don't want to share and that's fine! Don't feel bad about it. **3**

Nikolay, St Petersburg, Russia
It's not a good idea to wait for others to make you happy. There are times when you're happy, and other times when you're sad. And when you're not happy, try to think, 'What can I do to stop this? How can I help myself?' Friendship is a place to share **happiness**, but there may be times when you and your friends aren't happy. And that's OK. **5**

4 Read the web page again. Who says …

1 you need to have a good time with your friends?
_____

2 you won't make friends if you are an unfriendly person? _____

3 we need to remember that our friends have bad days too? _____

4 you don't have to tell your friends everything about you? _____

5 we won't always have the same number of friends in our life? _____

6 that it's not always a good thing to have a lot of friends? _____

7 we shouldn't expect our friends to always get everything right? _____

8 we shouldn't always expect friends to make us happy? _____

9 you can't always expect your friends to be happy?
_____

10 you can't make a really good friend quickly?
_____

5 VOCABULARY There are eight words in bold in the web page. Match the words with these meanings. Write the words.

0 an idea that many people believe, but that is not true _myth_

1 the state of feeling happy _____

2 the relationships you have with friends _____

3 show that you are not in a hurry and have got time _____

4 worried, for example when you have too much work _____

5 get to know and like a person _____

6 keep in your mind _____

7 at this moment _____

SPEAKING

1 Choose the words that make the sentences true for you.

1 When I'm sad, I want my friends to *listen to me / tell me a joke / leave me alone.*

2 When I'm happy, I want to *watch a film / play a sport / listen to music / go shopping /* with my friends.

2 Work with a partner. Read out your sentences and compare your answers.

WRITING
An apology

1 Read the message and answer the questions.

1 How does John feel and why?
2 What does he want to do about it?

Dear Alice,

I'm really sorry for forgetting your birthday. It was a terrible thing to do. I wanted to phone you but I forgot because I had a lot of work to do. I feel really bad. I'd like to see you soon to say sorry. I've also got something I want to give you.

Can we meet up on Thursday?

John

2 Read the messages. Which is the answer to John?

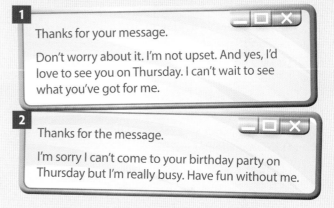

1

Thanks for your message.

Don't worry about it. I'm not upset. And yes, I'd love to see you on Thursday. I can't wait to see what you've got for me.

2

Thanks for the message.

I'm sorry I can't come to your birthday party on Thursday but I'm really busy. Have fun without me.

3 Put the words in the right order. Write the sentences.

1 birthday / your / really / sorry / for / I'm / forgetting
2 was / terrible / a / It / to / do / thing
3 really / I / bad / feel

4 Match the phrases with the photos.

eat the cake | break someone's tablet
not water the flowers

5 Write an apology for each photo. Include an explanation with each apology.
I'm really sorry.   It was an accident.

6 Choose one of the situations from above and write a message to apologise. (60 words)

CAMBRIDGE ENGLISH: Key

THiNK EXAMS

READING AND WRITING
Part 5: Multiple-choice cloze

Workbook page 53

1 Read the article about a strange house. Choose the best word (A, B or C) for each space.

I **(0)**_____ on holiday with my family in California a few years **(1)** _____ , when Dad saw an advert for 'The Craziest House in the World' in the local paper. We decided to visit it, but on the way there we got lost. Dad **(2)** _____ want to ask anyone for directions, but after half an hour Mum told him to stop. We found a really **(3)** _____ man on a street in the town. He **(4)** _____ us a map for free! And ten minutes later, we were at the house.

From the outside, it just looked **(5)** _____ a normal big house. When we went inside we saw how **(6)** _____ it was. The house has 40 bedrooms, three lifts, 47 fireplaces and 467 doors!

It was the project of a rich American woman called Sarah Winchester. They **(7)** _____ building it in 1884 and they only stopped in 1922 when Sarah died. She never drew any plans but every time she got **(8)** _____ with the house, she just called the builders to come and build some more rooms for her.

0	A am	B was	C were		
1	A last	B before	C ago		
2	A doesn't	B did	C didn't		
3	A helpful	B jealous	C confident		
4	A give	B gave	C giving		
5	A like	B at	C for		
6	A amazed	B relaxing	C amazing		
7	A start	B started	C starting		
8	A bored	B boring	C interesting		

(0 answer B was is circled)

Part 6: Word completion

Workbook page 43

2 Complete the words.

0 You usually keep your clothes in this.
  w a r d r o b e

1 You can keep your books on this. s _ _ _ _ _

2 You use this to look at yourself. m _ _ _ _ _ _

3 Someone who knows a lot of things is this.
  i _ _ _ _ _ _ _ _ _ _ _

4 Someone who always shares their things is this.
  g _ _ _ _ _ _ _

5 Someone who is relaxed and doesn't worry much is this. e _ _ _ - _ _ _ _ _

Part 3: Dialogue matching

Workbook page 35

3 Complete the conversation between two friends. What does Nick say to Sue? For questions 1–5, write the correct letter A–H in each space.

SUE   It's Adam's birthday next week.
NICK   **(0)** _F_
SUE   I think that's a great idea. But what?
NICK   **(1)** _____
SUE   I don't think that's a good idea. He doesn't like reading.
NICK   **(2)** _____
SUE   He downloads all his music. He hasn't even got a CD player.
NICK   **(3)** _____
SUE   I'm not so sure. It's difficult to buy clothes for him.
NICK   **(4)** _____
SUE   Let's invite him to the cinema. He loves films.
NICK   **(5)** _____
SUE   Great. I'll get three tickets.

A OK. Have you got any ideas?
B We could get him a CD. He loves music.
C Why don't we ask his dad?
D Let's do that.
E Why?
F ~~Why don't we get him a present?~~
G How about buying him a book?
H That's true. How about a T-shirt?

LISTENING
Part 2: Matching

Workbook page 61

4 ◀))2.02 Listen to Jen telling Mark about her room. Who gave her each of the pieces of furniture? For questions 1–5, write a letter A–H next to each present.

Present		People
0 armchair	E	A Dad
1 sofa	☐	B Uncle Tim
2 curtains	☐	C Aunt Abi
3 carpet	☐	D brother
4 desk	☐	E ~~Grandpa~~
5 lamp	☐	F Uncle Simon
		G Mark
		H Mum

TEST YOURSELF

VOCABULARY

1 **Use the words in the list to complete the sentences. There are two extra words.**

after | make | for | really | cheerful | do | annoying | shower | last | jealous | annoyed | cooker

1 She isn't happy when I see you. I think she's a bit _____ of you.
2 I need a wash but Ian is still in the _____ .
3 Mum died when I was 14 so I helped Dad look _____ my little brothers.
4 My sister borrowed my shoes and she didn't ask me. I was really _____ .
5 I moved school when I was eight and I found it really difficult to _____ new friends.
6 I'm looking _____ Anne. Do you know where she is?
7 He's a really _____ boy. I really don't like him.
8 I had a great time _____ night – thanks for everything.
9 It's a _____ comfortable armchair. I just want to sit in it for hours.
10 Be careful – the _____ is still hot.

/10

GRAMMAR

2 **Complete the sentences with the past form of the verbs in the list.**

choose | find | go | think | like | see

1 I _____ he was my friend but now I'm not so sure.
2 The present was very expensive. I hope she _____ it.
3 I _____ to a party last night and I only got home at 11 pm.
4 I liked the green T-shirt but eventually I _____ the red one.
5 We _____ a dog all alone in the street so we took it home.
6 No, not that film. I _____ it last week.

3 **Find and correct the mistake in each sentence.**

1 I thinked you were at school.
2 Did you enjoyed your meal, Sir?
3 Paul wasn't go to school today. He stayed at home.
4 We were tired so we did go to bed early.
5 Where did you and Lucy met?
6 I wasn't hungry so I didn't ate anything.

/12

FUNCTIONAL LANGUAGE

4 **Write the missing words.**

1 A How a_____ inviting Jake to our party?
  B I don't think that's a good i_____ . Remember the last time he went to a party!
2 A We c_____ have pizza for lunch.
  B Let's d_____ that. I love pizza!
3 A If you need some money, w_____ don't you get a Saturday job?
  B I'm not so s_____ . I don't think my dad would like it.
4 A L_____ go to the park after school.
  B That's a g_____ idea. We can play tennis.

/8

MY SCORE [ ] /30

| 22 – 30 |
| 10 – 21 |
| 0 – 9 |

PRONUNCIATION

UNIT 1
/s/, /z/, /ɪz/ sounds

1 **🔊 1.18 Listen to the sentences.**

Gus makes cakes and sweets. He works hard and sleeps a lot.
James enjoys all kinds of games. He plays a lot of football with his friends.
Liz's job is fun. She washes and brushes horses and relaxes by riding them.

2 **Say the words with the /s/, /z/ and /ɪz/ endings.**

3 **🔊 1.19 Listen and repeat. Then practise with a partner.**

UNIT 2
Contractions

1 **🔊 1.27 Listen to the dialogue.**

TOM   Here's your pizza, Jane.
JANE That's not my pizza. I don't like cheese.
TOM   But Jane! They've all got cheese!
JANE No they haven't. There's one without it.
TOM   You're right ... it's this one. Here you are.

2 **Say the words in blue.**

3 **🔊 1.28 Listen and repeat. Then practise with a partner.**

UNIT 3
Vowel sounds /ɪ/ and /iː/

1 **🔊 1.36 Listen to the tongue twisters.**

Jill wishes she had fish and chips for dinner.
Pete's eating meat with cheese and peas.
Pete and Jill drink tea with milk.

2 **Say the words with the short /ɪ/ sound. Say the words with the long /iː/ sound.**

3 **🔊 1.37 Listen and repeat. Then practise with a partner.**

UNIT 4
-er /ə/ at the end of words

1 **🔊 1.42 Listen to the tongue twister.**

Jennifer's father's a firefighter,
Oliver's mother's a travel writer,
Peter's sister's a lorry driver;
And Amber's brother's a deep-sea diver.

2 **Say the words with the weak -er sound (the schwa /ə/).**

3 **🔊 1.43 Listen and repeat. Then practise with a partner.**

UNIT 5
Regular past tense endings: /d/, /t/ and /ɪd/

1 **🔊 1.48 Listen to the dialogue.**

MUM   What happened in the kitchen, Jack? It's a mess!
JACK I started to make a cake; then I decided to make a pizza. I cooked all morning and cleaned all afternoon.
MUM   You cleaned? What did you clean?
JACK My bedroom!

2 **Say the past tense words with the /d/, /t/ and /ɪd/ endings.**

3 **🔊 1.49 Listen and repeat. Then practise with a partner.**

UNIT 6
Stressed syllables in words

1 **🔊 1.55 Listen to the sentences.**

Sarah's funny, cheerful and helpful.
Jonathan's generous, confident and talented.
Elizabeth's intelligent, adventurous and easy-going.

2 **Say the two, three and four syllable words. Stress the words correctly.**

3 **🔊 1.56 Listen and repeat. Then practise with a partner.**

GET IT RIGHT!

UNIT 1
Adverbs of frequency

> Words like *sometimes*, *never*, *always* come <u>between</u> the subject and the verb or adjective.
> ✓ I **sometimes do** my homework on Saturday.
> ✗ I ~~do sometimes~~ my homework on Saturday.

> **Correct the six adverbs that are in the wrong place.**
> I have always fun on Saturday! In the morning, I usually meet my friends in the park or they come sometimes to my house. In the afternoon, we go often swimming. I never do homework on Saturday. In the evening, we have always pizza. My mum usually cooks the pizza at home, but we go occasionally to a restaurant. I always am very tired on Sunday!

like + *-ing*

> We use the *-ing* form of the verb after verbs expressing likes and dislikes.
> ✓ He **likes watching** TV.   ✗ He ~~likes watch~~ TV.

> **Find five mistakes in the conversation. Correct them.**
> LUCY What do you like doing, Jim?
> JIM   I love play with my dog, Spud.
> LUCY Does he enjoy swim?
> JIM   No, he hates swim. But he likes go to the beach.
> LUCY I like play on the beach, too!

UNIT 2
Verbs of perception

> We use the present simple with verbs of perception (*look, taste, sound, smell*) to talk about something that is true now. We don't use the present continuous.
> ✓ His new jacket **looks terrible**!
> ✗ His new jacket ~~is looking terrible~~!

> We use *look, taste, sound, smell* + adjective, NOT *look, taste, sound, smell* + *like* + adjective.
> ✓ This pizza **tastes awful**!
> ✗ This pizza ~~tastes like awful~~!

> <u>Underline</u> **the correct sentence.**
> 1 a I think this jacket looks expensive.
>   b I think this jacket is looking expensive.
> 2 a Your weekend sounds great!
>   b Your weekend sounds like great!
> 3 a Look at that dog. He looks like happy.
>   b Look at that dog. He looks happy.
> 4 a The music is sounding beautiful.
>   b The music sounds beautiful.

Present continuous

> We form the present continuous with the present simple of *be* before the *-ing* form (e.g. *running, doing, wearing*, etc.) of the main verb, i.e. subject + *be* + *-ing* form of the verb.
> ✓ I **am looking** at the sky.
> ✗ ~~I looking~~ at the sky.

> But in questions, we use the present simple of *be* <u>before</u> the person doing the action, i.e. *be* + subject + *-ing* form of verb.
> ✓ **Why are you looking** at the sky?
> ✗ ~~Why you are looking~~ at the sky?

> **Put the correct form of *be* in the correct place in the sentences.**
> 1 What you looking at?
> 2 They going shopping today.
> 3 I looking for a new jacket.
> 4 She wearing a beautiful dress.
> 5 Why he laughing? It's not funny!

UNIT 3
much and *many*

> We use *many* with plural countable nouns and *much* with uncountable nouns.
> ✓ How **many** sandwiches have you got?
> ✗ How ~~much~~ sandwiches have you got?
> ✓ We haven't got **much** cheesecake.
> ✗ We haven't got ~~many~~ cheesecake.

Read the conversation. Circle *much* **or** *many*.

SARAH Hi, Julian, have we got everything we need for the party?

JULIAN We've got some crisps, but we haven't got ¹*many / much* fruit.

SARAH How ²*many / much* apples did you buy?

JULIAN We've got six apples, but we haven't got ³*many / much* vegetables.

SARAH I've got four tomatoes. How ⁴*many / much* people are coming?

JULIAN Everybody from our class is coming!

SARAH Oh, have we got ⁵*many / much* juice?

JULIAN Yes, but we haven't got ⁶*many / much* glasses.

SARAH Oh dear! We've got a problem.

too + adjective and (*not*) + adjective + *enough*

We use *too* + adjective to say there is more than is necessary of something. We never use *too much* + adjective.

✓ *The soup was **too cold**.*
✗ *The soup was* ~~too much cold~~.

We use *not* before the adjective and *enough* <u>after</u> the adjective to say there is less than is necessary of something.

✓ *The soup wasn't **hot enough**.*
✗ *The soup* ~~wasn't enough hot~~.

Write a cross (✗) next to the incorrect sentences. Then write the correct sentences.

1 We didn't go because the weather wasn't enough good.

2 The sausages were too spicy. And the pizza wasn't warm enough.

3 I didn't do my homework. I was too much tired.

4 The food he eats is healthy not enough.

5 The room wasn't enough big and the price was too much expensive.

UNIT 4
Possessive adjectives and pronouns

We don't use *a/an* or *the* before possessive adjectives or possessive pronouns.

✓ *This is **my sister**.*
✗ *This is* ~~the my sister~~.
✓ *This is **mine**. Where is **yours**?*
✗ *This is* ~~the mine~~. *Where is* ~~the yours~~?

Find five mistakes in the conversation. Correct them.

CLARA Hi Ben, is that your phone?

BEN No, it's a my brother's. His is black and the mine's blue. The one on the table is the mine.

CLARA Oh, it's great! I need a new phone. The mine is really old!

BEN When is your birthday? Maybe your mum will give you a new phone.

CLARA Hmm. But the my birthday is in December! I need a new phone now!

Possessive *'s*

We don't usually use noun + *of* + noun to talk about possession. We use name or noun + *'s*.

✓ *That is **my cousin's house**.*
✗ *That is* ~~the house of my cousin~~.

Rewrite these sentences using *'s*.

1 She's the sister of my best friend.

2 They are the grandparents of my cousin.

3 Is that the brother of your best friend?

4 She's the sister of my mum.

5 That's the phone of my brother.

you, *your* or *yours*?

We use *you* to refer to the subject or object. We use *your* to talk about possession.

✓ *Thank you very much for **your letter**.*
✗ *Thank you very much for* ~~you letter~~.

We use *your* before a noun for possession. We use *yours* to replace *your* + noun.

✓ *Is this **your phone**?* ✓ *Is this **phone yours**?*
✗ *Is this* ~~yours phone~~?

⟨Circle⟩ the correct word to complete the letter.

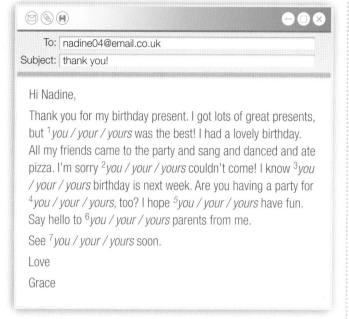

To: nadine04@email.co.uk
Subject: thank you!

Hi Nadine,

Thank you for my birthday present. I got lots of great presents, but ¹*you / your / yours* was the best! I had a lovely birthday. All my friends came to the party and sang and danced and ate pizza. I'm sorry ²*you / your / yours* couldn't come! I know ³*you / your / yours* birthday is next week. Are you having a party for ⁴*you / your / yours*, too? I hope ⁵*you / your / yours* have fun. Say hello to ⁶*you / your / yours* parents from me.

See ⁷*you / your / yours* soon.

Love

Grace

UNIT 5
Modifiers: *quite, very, really*

> **Remember: we use modifier + adjective (+ noun). We don't use noun + modifier + adjective.**
>
> ✓ *Pompeii has **a lot of very old buildings**.*
> ✗ *Pompeii has a lot of ~~buildings very old~~.*
> ✓ *The buildings are **very old**.*
>
> **Be careful when you write these words.**
>
> - **We write *quite* with the e <u>after</u> the t. Don't confuse *quite* with the adjective *quiet*.**
>   ✓ *This chair is **quite** comfortable.*
>   ✗ *This chair is ~~quiet~~ comfortable.*
> - **We write *really* with two *lls*.**
>   ✓ *Pompeii is **really** interesting.*
>   ✗ *Pompeii is ~~realy~~ interesting.*
> - **We write *very* with one *r*.**
>   ✓ *Their house is **very** big.*
>   ✗ *Their house is ~~verry~~ big.*

Find seven mistakes. Correct them.

We went to see our new house on Sunday. My dad wants to live near his office. It's realy annoying for me because a lot of my friends live near my house now. I was very sad when we went into the house. But when I saw inside it, I was amazed really! It looked quiet small, but inside it was really big. It had a kitchen really big and the bedrooms were verry big too. But the best thing was the garden. It was beautiful really, with a swimming pool very big and lots of trees. I think my friends will like visiting my new house!

UNIT 6
Past simple (regular and irregular verbs)

> **To make any verb negative in the past simple we use *didn't* + the base form of the verb. We don't use *didn't* + past simple. Remember to use the base form of regular and irregular verbs.**
>
> ✓ *We **didn't visit** the Lego house.*
> ✗ *We ~~didn't visited~~ the Lego house.*

⟨Circle⟩ the correct answer.

1 I'm sorry I didn't *come / came* to your party.
2 We didn't *went / go* on holiday last year.
3 I looked everywhere, but I didn't *found / find* my phone.
4 We visited the art gallery but we didn't *see / saw* anything interesting.
5 We didn't *spend / spent* a lot of time in Paris. It was too hot!
6 I didn't *knew / know* you liked One Direction.

Double genitive

> **We form the double genitive with noun + *of* + possessive pronoun (*mine, yours, his, hers, ours, yours, theirs*). We don't use object pronouns (*me, you, him, her, our, your, their*) to form the double genitive.**
>
> ✓ *She's a **friend of mine**.*
> ✗ *She's a friend ~~of me~~.*
>
> **We also form the double genitive with noun + *of* + possessive adjective (*my, your, his, her, our, your, their*) + noun + possessive *'s*.**
>
> ✓ *She's a **friend of my sister's**.*
> ✗ *She's a friend ~~of my sister~~.*

⟨Circle⟩ the correct answer.

1 Lisa is a good friend of *me / my / mine*.
2 Matt Damon is a favourite actor of my *sister / sister's*.
3 My brother went to the cinema with a friend of *him / he's / his*.
4 I met a cousin of *Rory's / Rory* at the party.
5 She brought a new classmate of *hers / her / she's* to the party.
6 Isn't that woman a teacher of *your / you / yours*?

This page is intentionally left blank.

STUDENT A

UNIT 2, PAGE 23

Student A

1 You are a customer in a sports shop. You like a
pair of trainers.
You want a black pair.
You want to know the price.
You want to try them on.

2 You are an assistant in a clothes shop. Student B
likes a sweatshirt. It's €36.95. You have green,
blue or red.

UNIT 5, PAGE 55

Student A

You and your friend have got £200. You are at a flea
market buying furniture for a new room for your youth
club. These are the prices of the pieces of furniture:

- 2 armchairs £30
- cooker £20
- shelf £5
- table with 8 chairs £70
- desk and lamp £25
- sofa £75
- large carpet £70
- mirror £10
- wardrobe £30
- small carpet £30
- sofa £40
- 8 posters of film stars £5

You want to buy the 2 armchairs, the large carpet, the
cooker and the posters.

You do not want to buy the shelf or the wardrobe.

You are uncertain about the table with the 8 chairs
and the sofas.

Have a conversation and agree on what to buy.

STUDENT B

UNIT 2, PAGE 23

Student B

1   You are an assistant in a sports shop.
Student A likes a pair of trainers. They're €34.99.
You only have brown or red (not black).

2   You are a customer in a clothes shop. You like
a sweatshirt.

You want a green one.

You want to know the price.

You want to try it on.

UNIT 5, PAGE 55

Student B

You and your friend have got £200. You are at a flea
market buying furniture for a new room for your youth
club. These are the prices of the pieces of furniture:

- 2 armchairs £30
- cooker £20
- shelf £5
- table with 8 chairs £70
- desk and lamp £25
- sofa £75
- large carpet £70
- mirror £10
- wardrobe £30
- small carpet £30
- sofa £40
- 8 posters of film stars £5

You want to buy the table with the 8 chairs, the
cooker, the large carpet, and one of the sofas.

You do not want to buy the 2 armchairs or the posters.

You are uncertain about the desk and the lamp.

Have a conversation and agree on what to buy.

Acknowledgements

The authors and publishers acknowledge the following sources of copyright material and are grateful for the permissions granted. While every effort has been made, it has not always been possible to identify the sources of all the material used, or to trace all copyright holders. If any omissions are brought to our notice, we will be happy to include the appropriate acknowledgements on reprinting.

The publishers are grateful to the following for permission to reproduce copyright photographs and material:

T = Top, B = Below, L = Left, R = Right, C = Centre, B/G = Background

p. 4 (L): ©Odilon Dimier/PhotoAlto/Corbis; p. 4 (1-12): ©Laschon Robert Paul/Shutterstock; p. 5 (0): ©lazyllama/Shutterstock; p. 5 (1): ©Plush Studios/Blend Images/360/Getty Images; p. 5 (2): ©Shelly Perry/iStock/360/Getty Images; p. 5 (3): ©Dmitry Shabanov/age fotostock/Superstock; p. 5 (4): ©Jose Luis Pelaez Inc/Blend Images/Corbis; p. 5 (5): ©Chris Rout/Alamy; p. 5 (6): ©George Doyle/Stockbyte/Getty Images; p. 5 (7): ©Jupiterimages/Photos.com/360/Getty Images; p. 5 (8): ©blackdovfx/iStock/360/Getty Images; p. 5 (9): ©moodboard/360/Getty Images; p. 8 (TL): ©Camilla Morandi/REX; p. 8 (TR): ©Ken McKay/REX; p. 8 (CL): ©David Ramos/Getty Images News/Getty Images; p. 8 (CR): ©Quinn Rooney/Getty Images Sport/Getty Images; p. 8 (BL): ©Action Press/REX; p. 8 (BR): ©David Buchan/Getty Images Entertainment/Getty Images; p. 9 (Ex7 a): ©DAJ/Getty Images; p. 9 (Ex7 b): ©Ben Molyneux People/Alamy; p. 9 (Ex7 c): ©Juanmonino/iStock/360/Getty Images; p. 9 (Ex7 d): ©monkeybusinessimages/iStock/Thinkstock/Getty Images; p. 9 (Ex7 e): ©Juice Images/Juice Images/Superstock; p. 9 (Ex7 f): ©Fuse/Getty Images; p. 9 (Ex7 g): ©Pixland/360/Getty Images; p. 9 (Ex7 h): ©altrendo images/Altrendo/Getty Images; p. 9 (Ex9 a): ©Nikolai Sorokin/Hemera/360/Getty Images; p. 9 (Ex9 b): ©Natalia Siverina/Hemera/360/Getty Images; p. 9 (Ex9 c): ©murat sengul/iStock/360/Getty Images; p. 9 (Ex9 d): ©P P/Hemera/360/Getty Images; p. 9 (Ex9 e): ©Lisa Quarfoth/Hemera/360/Getty Images; p. 9 (Ex9 f): ©lucato/iStock/360/Getty Images; p. 9 (Ex9 g): ©P P/Hemera/360/Getty Images; p. 9 (Ex9 h): ©Tatiana Grinberg/Hemera/360/Getty Images; p. 10 (cat): ©perfectescape/iStock/360/Getty Images; p. 10 (lizard): ©vladimirts/iStock/360/Getty Images; p. 10 (phone): ©Grassetto/iStock/360/Getty Images; p. 10 (MP3): ©djem/Shutterstock; p. 10 (tablet): ©daboost/iStock/360/Getty Images; p. 10 (TV): ©ISerg/iStock/360/Getty Images; p. 10 (bike): ©arquiplay77/iStock/360/Getty Images; p. 10 (camera): ©Evgeny Karandaev/Shutterstock; p. 11 (TL): ©Robert Kent/Compassionate Eye Foundation/Photdisc/Getty Images; p. 11 (TC): ©BestPhotoStudio/Shutterstock; p. 11 (BL): ©mandymin/iStock/360/Getty Images; p. 11 (BC): ©Darren Robb/The Image Bank/Getty Images; p. 11 (R): ©Photographee.eu/Shutterstock; p. 12 (a): ©diego_cervo/iStock/360/Getty Images; p. 12 (b): ©wavebreakmedia/Shutterstock; p. 12 (c): ©lsantilli/Shutterstock; p. 12 (d): ©Digital Vision/Getty Images; p. 12 (e): ©R. Gino Santa Maria/Shutterstock; p. 12 (f): ©Marc Debnam/Photodisc/Getty Images; p. 12 (g): ©Chad Baker/Jason Reed/Ryan McVay/Photodisc/Getty Images; p. 12 (h): ©ALAN EDWARDS/Alamy; p. 13 (a): ©Holloway/Stone/Getty Images; p. 13 (b): ©Aleksandr Markin/Shutterstock; p. 13 (c): ©Domino/The Image Bank/Getty Images; p. 13 (d): ©PathDoc/Shutterstock; p. 13 (e): ©Ashley Whitworth/iStock/360/Getty Images; p. 13 (f): ©PaulMaguire/iStock/360/Getty Images; p. 13 (g): ©Mark Bowden/Getty Images; p. 14 (L): ©Jim West/Alamy; p. 14 (C): ©ewa galus/Shutterstock; p. 14 (R): ©Peeradach Rattanakoses/Shutterstock; p. 15 (L): ©Matt Antonino/Shutterstock; p. 15 (R): ©Linda Patterson/Design Pics/Design Pics/Corbis; p. 16 (T): ©Emilio Ereza/Alamy; p. 16 (BL): ©Linda Armstrong/Shutterstock; p. 16 (BR): ©monkeybusinessimages/iStock/360/Getty Images; p. 20 (a): ©Polryaz/Shutterstock; p. 20 (b): ©Ekaterina Kamenetsky/Shutterstock; p. 20 (c): ©scanrail/iStock/360/Getty Images; p. 20 (d): ©Duygun VURALI/iStock/360/Getty Images; p. 20 (e): ©_human/iStock/360/Getty Images; p. 20 (f): ©stockcreations/Shutterstock; p. 22 (1): ©incamerastock/Alamy; p. 22 (2): ©Adisa/Shutterstock; p. 22 (3, 4): ©Jupiterimages/Polka Dot/360/Getty Images; p. 22 (5): ©Ian G Dagnall/Alamy; p. 22 (6): ©Jiri Hubatka/Alamy; p. 22 (7): ©British Retail Photography/Alamy; p. 22 (8): ©Guy Somerset/Alamy; p. 23 (a): ©kaktyc/iStock/360/Getty Images; p. 23 (b): ©LuminaStock/iStock/360/Getty Images; p. 23 (c): ©RusN/iStock/360/Getty Images; p. 23 (d): ©samsonovs/iStock/360/Getty Images; p. 24 (0): ©vladislav mitic/iStock/360/Getty Images; p. 24 (1): ©Karkas/Shutterstock; p. 24 (2): ©bergamont/iStock/360/Getty Images; p. 24 (3): ©graphicdna/iStock/360/Getty Images; p. 24 (4): ©Olga Popova/iStock/360/Getty Images; p. 24 (5): ©roibu/iStock/360/Getty Images; p. 24 (6): ©Evgeniy Pavlenko/iStock/360/Getty Images; p. 24 (7): ©jitalia17/iStock/360/Getty Images; p. 24 (8): ©shippee/iStock/360/Getty Images; p. 24 (9): ©Elnur/Shutterstock; p. 25 (L): ©Startraks Photo/REX; p. 25 (R): ©REX; p. 26 (a): ©YOSHIKAZU TSUNO/AFP/Getty Images; p. 26 (b): ©EvrenKalinbacak/iStock/360/Getty Images; p. 26 (c): ©Peter Phipp/Travelshots.com/Alamy; p. 26 (d): ©David Kilpatrick/Alamy; p. 26 (e): ©Geraint Lewis/Alamy; p. 31 (TR): ©bokan/Shutterstock; p. 31 (BL): ©AFP/Getty Images; p. 31 (BR, B/G): ©Maksim Aan/Shutterstock; p. 32 (1): ©valery121283/iStock/360/Getty Images; p. 32 (2, 6, 9): ©Joe Gough/iStock/360/Getty Images; p. 32 (3): ©slav/iStock/360/Getty Images; p. 32 (4): ©Leonid Nyshko/iStock/360/Getty Images; p. 32 (5): ©voltan1/iStock/360/Getty Images; p. 32 (7): ©Florin1605/iStock/360/Getty Images; p. 32 (8): ©thumb/iStock/360/Getty Images; p. 32 (10): ©GooDween123/iStock/360/Getty Images; p. 34: ©Alija/Vetta/Getty Images; p. 35 (a): ©arnoaltix/iStock/360/Getty Images; p. 35 (b): ©foodfolio/Alamy; p. 35 (c): ©Profimedia.CZ a.s./Alamy; p. 35 (d): ©schulzie/iStock/360/Getty Images; p. 38: ©Comstock Images/Stockbyte/Getty Images; p. 39 (TL): ©20TH CENTURY FOX/THE KOBAL COLLECTION/GROENING, MATT; p. 39 (TR): ©Everett Collection/REX; p. 39 (B): ©COLOR FORCE/FOX 2000 PICTURES/TCF/THE KOBAL COLLECTION; p. 42 (L): ©T.J. Hamilton/AP/Press Association Images, p. 42 (R). ©Zoonar/Zoonar/360/Getty Images; p. 44 (TR): ©Koichi Kamoshida/Getty Images News/Getty Images; p. 44 (C): ©Dawn Hudson/iStock/360/Getty Images; p. 44 (BL): ©Dorothy Alexander/Alamy; p. 48 (TL, BC): ©Lisa Turay/iStock/360/Getty Images; p. 48 (TC): ©View Pictures Ltd/Superstock; p. 48 (TR): ©Michael Higginson/iStock/360/Getty Images; p. 48 (BL): ©KatarzynaBialasiewicz/iStock/360/Getty Images; p. 48 (BR): ©Artazum and Iriana Shiyan/Shutterstock; p. 49 (L): ©Steve Parsons/PA Archive/Press Association Images; p. 49 (R): ©James Boardman/Alamy; p. 50 (a): ©darksite/iStock/360/Getty Images; p. 50 (b): ©Milan Vasicek/iStock/360/Getty Images; p. 50 (c): ©AnnaDavy/iStock/360/Getty Images; p. 50 (d): ©DusanTomic/iStock/360/Getty Images; p. 50 (e): ©jur_ziv/Shutterstock; p. 50 (f): ©Africa Studio/Shutterstock; p. 50 (g): ©photobac/iStock/360/Getty Images; p. 50 (h): ©Antonio Gravante/iStock/360/Getty Images; p. 50 (i): ©MISCELLANEOUSTOCK/Alamy; p. 50 (j): ©ppart/iStock/360/Getty Images; p. 50 (k): ©janniwet/iStock/360/Getty Images; p. 50 (l): ©terekhov igor/Shutterstock; p. 52 (T): ©Natalia Lukiyanova/iStock/360/Getty Images; p. 52 (CL): ©Enrico Della Pietra/Alamy; p. 52 (CR): ©Heritage Image Partnership Ltd/Alamy; p. 52 (B): ©PRISMA ARCHIVO/Alamy; p. 56 (TL): ©Rido/Shutterstock; p. 56 (TC): ©Neustockimages/Vetta/Getty Images; p. 56 (BC): ©Ableimages/Digital Vision/Getty Images; p. 56 (R): ©Leanne Temme/Photolibrary/Getty Images; p. 57 (T): ©MediaPunch/REX; p. 57 (B): ©Ken McKay/REX; p. 59: ©Paul Gilham/Getty Images; p. 60 (TL): ©Radius Images/Alamy; p. 60 (TR): ©Masson/Shutterstock; p. 60 (B): ©danbreckwoldt/iStock/360/Getty Images; p. 62 (TR): ©Fuse/Getty Images; p. 62 (L): ©Goodshoot/360/Getty Images; p. 62 (BR): ©Elena Elisseeva/iStock/360/Getty Images; p. 63 (L): ©gunnarAssmy/iStock/360/Getty Images; p. 63 (C): ©xrrr/iStock/360/Getty Images; p. 63 (R): ©D.Trozzo/Alamy.

Commissioned photography by: Jon Barlow p 18, 36, 54.

Cover photographs by: : (L): ©Yuliya Koldovska/Shutterstock; (TR): ©Tim Gainey/Alamy; (BR): ©Oliver Burston/Alamy.

The publishers are grateful to the following illustrators: Fred Van Deelen (The Organisation) 6, 21, 28, 30, 51; Laura Martinez (Sylvie Poggio Artists Agency) 7, 8, 41, 53; David Semple 15, 19, 25, 37, 43; Bryan Beach (Advocate Art) 40; Seb Camagajevac (Beehive Illustration) 58; Paul Hostetler 61

The publishers are grateful to the following contributors: Blooberry: text design and layouts; Claire Parson: cover design; Hilary Fletcher: picture research; Leon Chambers: audio recordings; Silversun Media Group: video production; Karen Elliott: Pronunciation sections; Diane Nicholls: Get it right! section

This page is intentionally left blank.

WORKBOOK 1

A2

Herbert Puchta, Jeff Stranks & Peter Lewis-Jones

CAMBRIDGE
UNIVERSITY PRESS

This page is intentionally left blank.

CONTENTS

WELCOME

A ALL ABOUT ME
Personal information

1 Match the sentences and the replies.

1	What's your name? ☐	a	I'm 14.
2	How old are you? ☐	b	Hi, Lucy, I'm Laura.
3	Where are you from? ☐	c	Hi, Jim. Nice to meet you.
4	Hi, I'm Lucy. ☐	d	Nice to meet you, too.
5	This is my friend Jim. ☐	e	My name's Steve.
6	Nice to meet you. ☐	f	I'm from Hereford in England.

2 Write <u>your</u> answers to questions 1–3 in Exercise 1.

1 _____

2 _____

3 _____

Nationalities and *be*

1 Find 12 countries in the word search.

```
T C O L O M B I A O N
K J C M Z F I U A R E
A R G E N T I N A Y T
T K T X T Y U O U E H
L N U I K L U Y W A E
P I R C O L U M B I R
N A K O A Y I E J S L
C T E U P L P W N S A
X I Y S P A I N F U N
A R N A U T T M P R D
O B R A Z I L D M O S
P A L R M U I G L E B
```

2 Complete with the verb *to be*.

0 It *'s* a Ferrari.

1 They _____ from Moscow.

2 I _____ (not) from London.

3 _____ Paula from New York?

4 _____ you from São Paulo?

5 We _____ (not) from Barcelona.

6 Augusto _____ from a small town near Buenos Aires.

7 My dad _____ (not) from Rome.

3 Match the sentences 0–7 in Exercise 2 with a–h.

a We're from Madrid. ☐

b They're Russian. ☐

c He's Argentinian. ☐

d But he is Italian. ☐

e Yes, I'm Brazilian. ☐

f It's an Italian car. ☐

g I'm from Liverpool. ☐

h Yes, she's American. ☐

4 Write the nationality of someone from ...

1 The Netherlands _____

2 Colombia _____

3 Mexico _____

4 Belgium _____

5 Turkey _____

6 Brazil _____

7 Argentina _____

8 Russia _____

9 Italy _____

10 The USA _____

11 Britain _____

12 Spain _____

Names and addresses

1 🔊02 Listen to the telephone conversation. Who is the man calling?

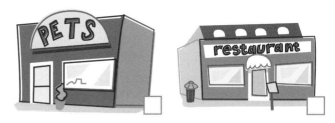

2 🔊02 **Listen again and complete the form.**

The Golden Duck

Table for: ¹ _____

Time: ² _____

Name: ³ _____

Contact number: ⁴ _____

⁵ _____ City Walls Road

3 🔊02 **Put the dialogue in order. Listen again and check.**

	MANAGER	OK, Mr Hodgson. And can I have a contact number?
	MANAGER	Sure, it's 22 City Walls Road.
	MANAGER	Could you spell that?
1	MANAGER	The Golden Duck. How can I help you?
	MANAGER	A table for four at 8 pm. Can I have your name?
	MANAGER	Thank you. See you later tonight, Mr Hodgson.
	MR HODGSON	Just one more thing. Can you give me your address?
	MR HODGSON	It's Hodgson. Bob Hodgson.
	MR HODGSON	Sure. It's H - O - D - G - S - O - N.
	MR HODGSON	Hello, I'd like to book a table for four for tonight about 8 pm.
	MR HODGSON	Yes, it's 0796 38888.

SUMMING UP

1 Complete the text with the verb *to be* and the nationalities.

My favourite football team has players in it from all over the world.
Costa and Nunes ¹_____ from Rio de Janeiro.
They ²_____ ³_____ .
Ramos ⁴_____ from Bogotá. He ⁵_____
⁶_____ .
Simenon ⁷_____ ⁸_____ . He ⁹_____
from Brussels.
Jones and Lalas ¹⁰_____ ¹¹_____ . Jones
¹²_____ from New York and Lalas ¹³_____
from Miami.
The other players ¹⁴_____ ¹⁵_____ . They
¹⁶_____ from lots of different cities in Britain.

B WHAT'S THAT?
Things in the classroom and prepositions of place

1 Find and circle 12 classroom items in the word snake.

2 Complete with the classroom objects in the list.

ruler | teacher | chair | pen | board | notebook

1 The _____ is under the chair.
2 The _____ is behind the desk.
3 The _____ is on the desk.
4 The _____ is in front of the board.
5 The _____ is between the door and the window.
6 The _____ is on a book.

Classroom language

1 **Put the words in order to make sentences.**

1 I / a / can / question /ask / ?

_____

2 again / can / say / that / you / ?

_____

3 page / your / open / at / 10 / books

_____

4 don't / I / know

_____

5 I / understand / don't

_____

6 mean / word / does / what / this / ?

_____

7 that / do / word / spell / you / how / ?

_____

8 English / how / say / *amanhã* / in / do / you / ?

_____

9 if / hands / your / know / up / answer / put / you / the

_____

Object pronouns

1 **Complete the table.**

I	*me*
you	_____
he	_____
she	_____
it	_____
we	_____
they	_____

2 **Circle the correct options in each sentence.**

0 May's my best friend. I tell *she / her* everything.

1 *They / Them* don't speak English. That's why you don't understand *they / them*.

2 *I / Me* love this dress. Buy it for *I / me*, please.

3 Turn the music up. *We / Us* can't hear it.

4 Bob's got a problem and *I / me* can't help *he / him*.

5 *We / Us* love our gran. She gives *we / us* great presents on our birthdays.

3 **Complete with the missing object pronoun.**

0 I want my sandwich! Give it to ___*me*___.

1 That's Mr O'Brian. Say hello to _____.

2 Mum wants some help. Can you help _____?

3 I love _____. You're my best friend.

4 We really want to go to the show. Can you buy _____ some tickets?

5 The children are very noisy. Tell _____ to be quiet, please.

this, that, these, those

1 **Circle the right words.**

1 *This / These* homework is very difficult.

2 *That / Those* shoes are really nice.

3 *That / These* house is really old.

4 *These / This* books aren't very interesting.

2 **Complete with *this, that, these* or *those*.**

1 Can you pass me _____ books next to you, please?

2 Is _____ my pen in your hand?

3 _____ pencil is broken. Can you give me another one?

4 _____ shoes are too small for me. I need to take them off.

SUMMING UP

1 **Complete the dialogue with the words in the list.**

~~ask~~ | know | spell | this | that
pen | say | notebook | put

ROBERTO   Excuse me, Miss Baker, can I [0] ___*ask*___ you a question?

MISS BAKER   Of course you can, Roberto.

ROBERTO   How do you [1]_____ 'pizza' in English?

MISS BAKER   Ahmed. Can you help?

AHMED   Sorry. I don't [2]_____ .

MISS BAKER   Can anyone help Roberto? [3]_____ your hands up if you know the answer. Yes, Kim.

KIM   It's easy. It's 'pizza'.

ROBERTO   How do you [4]_____ that?

KIM   P-I-Z-Z-A; it's the same as in Italian!

ROBERTO   OK, let me write that in my [5]_____ . Is [6]_____ your [7]_____? Can I borrow it?

KIM   No, [8]_____ 's your pen. You don't need to ask.

C ABOUT TIME

Days and dates

1 Sort the words into three different groups. There are four words in each group.

Sunday | October | fourteenth | third | July
Monday | second | tenth | March | Saturday
September | Friday

1 _____

2 _____

3 _____

2 Write the next word in each sequence.

1 February, April, June, _____

2 Friday, Thursday, Wednesday, _____

3 first, third, sixth, _____

4 1st, 10th, 19th, _____

5 April, August, December, _____

6 4th, 8th, 12th, _____

7 Monday, Wednesday, Friday, _____

8 December, November, October, _____

3 Write the numbers in words.

1 1st _____

2 4th _____

3 8th _____

4 11th _____

5 12th _____

6 15th _____

7 20th _____

8 22nd _____

9 25th _____

10 29th _____

11 30th _____

12 31st _____

4 Answer the questions.

When is …

1 your birthday?

_____

2 your country's national day?

_____

3 your best friend's birthday?

_____

4 the first day of your next school holiday?

_____

My day

1 Write the times on the clocks.

0 It's ___*4 pm.*___   1 It's _____

2 It's _____   3 It's _____

4 It's _____   5 It's _____

2 Read and put the events in order.

☐ I have lunch at quarter past one.

☐ I go to bed at twenty past eight.

☐ I go to school at seven o'clock.

☐ I have dinner at half past five.

☐ I have breakfast at quarter past six.

☐ I get home at half past one.

1 I get up at six o'clock.

☐ I do my homework at quarter to two.

3 Now write about your day.

1 *I get up at …* _____

2 _____

3 _____

4 _____

5 _____

6 _____

7 _____

8 _____

SUMMING UP

1 🔊 **03** **Listen and write the times that Dan does the following things.**

1 get up on Tuesday morning

_____

2 arrive at school

_____

3 get home after school

_____

4 go to bed

_____

5 get up on Sunday morning

_____

2 🔊 **03** **Put the dialogue in order. Listen and check.**

	ANA	What!? Six o'clock!
	ANA	Half past six in the morning? That's early. Why?
	ANA	Oh. And what time does it finish?
	ANA	So you love the weekend. You can get up late.
	ANA	What do you do after lunch?
1	ANA	What time do you get up, Dan?
	DAN	Yes, six o'clock. I have early morning swimming lessons.
	DAN	I do homework and watch TV. Sometimes I play football and basketball. Then it's dinner and I go to bed at nine o'clock.
	DAN	Well, my school starts at seven o'clock.
	DAN	Not at all. On Saturdays and Sundays I get up at six o'clock.
	DAN	From Monday to Friday, I get up at half past six.
	DAN	Twenty past twelve, so I get home at ten to one for lunch.

D MY THINGS
My possessions

1 Do the word puzzle and find the name of Jim's pet.

have got

1 Complete the sentences about Jim with *has* or *hasn't*. Use the previous exercise to help you.

1 Jim _____ got a lizard.

2 Jim _____ got a camera.

3 Jim _____ got a smartphone.

4 Jim _____ got a bike.

5 Jim _____ got a dog.

6 Jim _____ got a car.

2 Match the questions and the answers.

1 Have you got a pet? ☐

2 Has Jim got a cat? ☐

3 Have all your friends got smartphones? ☐

4 Has your brother got a bike? ☐

5 Have you got a lizard? ☐

6 Has Suzie got a brother? ☐

a Yes, they have.

b Yes, I've got a dog.

c No, he hasn't.

d No, she hasn't, but she's got a sister.

e No, I haven't.

f Yes, he has. It's called Mickey.

3 Circle the correct option.

1 I *have / has* got three brothers.

2 We *haven't / hasn't* got a car.

3 Susie *has / have* got a new phone.

4 They *haven't / hasn't* got any money.

5 James *haven't / hasn't* got homework tonight.

6 I *haven't / hasn't* got a pen. *Have / Has* you got one?

4 Complete the dialogue with *have*, *has*, *haven't* or *hasn't*.

BOB   ¹_____ you got a laptop, Nick?

NICK   No, I ²_____ but I'd love one.

BOB   What about your brother? ³_____ he got one?

NICK   Yes he ⁴_____ and he ⁵_____ got a tablet too.

BOB   That's not fair.

NICK   He's older than me. My sister ⁶_____ got one but she's only three.

BOB   ⁷_____ your parents got a computer?

NICK   Yes, they ⁸_____ . I use it sometimes.

5 Write sentences.

1 Two things you have got and two things you haven't got.

   _____

   _____

   _____

   _____

2 Two things your best friend has got and two things he/she hasn't got.

   _____

   _____

   _____

   _____

I like and *I'd like*

1 Circle the correct option.

1 A What's your favourite colour?

   B I *like / 'd like* blue best.

2 A Can I help you?

   B Yes, I *like / 'd like* an ice cream, please.

3 A What do you want to do?

   B I *like / 'd like* to play computer games.

4 A Do you want milk or orange juice?

   B I *like / 'd like* milk, please.

5 A Who's the best teacher at your school?

   B I *like / 'd like* Miss Dawes the most.

6 A Which day of the week do you like the most?

   B I *like / ' d like* Fridays.

7 A Do you want anything to eat?

   B I *like / 'd like* some chicken soup, please.

8 A What do you do in your free time?

   B I *like / 'd like* swimming and playing football.

SUMMING UP

1 Complete the mini dialogues with the missing questions.

1 A _____ ?

   B Yes, I'd love a dog or cat.

2 A _____ ?

   B No, I don't. I don't like any sports.

3 A _____ ?

   B Yes, I am. Very. I'd love a sandwich please.

4 A _____ ?

   B Yes, I do. Especially bananas and apples.

5 A _____ ?

   B Yes, I have. I've got a brother and two sisters.

6 A _____ ?

   B No, Rob hasn't got a cat but I think he's got a lizard.

7 A _____ ?

   B Yes, please. I'd love a glass of water. I'm really thirsty.

8 A _____ ?

   B No, we haven't got a car but we've all got bikes.

9 A _____ ?

   B Yes, I love dogs. We've got two.

10 A _____ ?

   B No, I haven't got a camera but I've got a smartphone.

1 | HAVING FUN

GRAMMAR
Present simple `SB p.14`

1 ★ ☆ ☆ **Circle** the correct option.

0   My mum *go /* *goes* to work by car.
1   He *think / thinks* I'm crazy.
2   Jim *look / looks* quite angry.
3   Dad *wash / washes* his car every Sunday.
4   I *doesn't / don't* feel very good.
5   Joe *doesn't / don't* want to have a shower now.
6   We *doesn't / don't* live very close to our school.

2 ★★ ☆ **Rewrite the sentences. Make the positive sentences negative. Make the negative sentences positive.**

0   Sally doesn't watch a lot of TV.
    Sally watches a lot of TV.

1   I like dancing.
    _____

2   Tim plays the guitar in a band.
    _____

3   Kelly doesn't miss her family a lot.
    _____

4   My parents work at the weekend.
    _____

3 ★★ ☆ **Use the words to write questions in the present simple.**

0   where / you / live?
    Where do you live?

1   you / speak / French?
    _____

2   what / your mum / do?
    _____

3   your teacher / give you / lots of homework?
    _____

4   what / bands / you / like?
    _____

5   you / play / instrument?
    _____

4 ★★ ☆ **Match the questions in Exercise 3 with the answers below.**

a   She's a businesswoman. ☐
b   Yes, I do. The piano. ☐
c   Just outside of London. ☐ *0*
d   Yes, she does. Every day. ☐
e   No, I don't. ☐
f   I don't really like music. ☐

5 ★★★ **Write answers to the questions in Exercise 3 so they are true for you.**

0   _____
1   _____
2   _____
3   _____
4   _____
5   _____

6 ★★★ **Read about Brian's hobby. Complete the text with the correct form of the words in the list.**

~~not collect~~ | stand | phone | see | write | say
tell | turn | not think | not do | not play | try

My friend Brian has a really unusual hobby. He
⁰*doesn't collect* stamps and he ¹_____ the
piano. No, these are normal hobbies. Brian's hobby
is really strange. My friend Brian's hobby is being on
TV. Every time he ²_____ a TV cameraman
and presenter in town he ³_____ behind the
presenter and ⁴_____ to appear on TV.

Then he ⁵_____ me and ⁶_____ me
to watch the news on TV. So I ⁷_____ on the
TV and there he is. He ⁸_____ anything silly.
He's just there smiling. Then he ⁹_____ about
it on his blog. He ¹⁰_____ he's famous. I
¹¹_____ he's famous, just a bit crazy!

Pronunciation

Plurals and third person verb endings:
/s/, /z/ or /ɪz/

Go to page 118. 🔊

---

like + -ing SB p.17

7 ★★☆ **Complete the sentences with the verbs in the list.**

~~take~~ | read | get | chat | go | do | help | tidy

Best and worst things to do on a Saturday morning.

0   I love _taking_ my dog for a walk.
1   I enjoy _____ Dad make breakfast.
2   I like _____ for a bike ride with my friends.
3   I love _____ a book in bed.
4   I enjoy _____ to my friends on the phone.
5   I hate _____ my homework.
6   I can't stand _____ up my bedroom.
7   I hate _____ out of bed before midday.

8 ★★★ **What about you? What do you like (and hate) doing on Saturday mornings? Complete the sentences so they are true for you.**

1   I love _____
2   I enjoy _____
3   I like _____
4   I hate _____
5   I can't stand _____

Adverbs of frequency SB p.17

9 ★☆☆ **Match the particles in the list to make adverbs of frequency and write them in the correct place.**

occasion	ten	100% _____
ne	ways	↑ _____
rare	times	↑ _____
some	ally	↑ _____
al	ly	↑ _____
usu	ally	↑ _____
of	ver	0% _____

10 ★★☆ **Rewrite the sentences with the adverb of frequency in the correct place.**

0   I play computer games after dinner. (usually)
   I usually play computer games after dinner.
1   You are happy. (always)
   _____
2   My best friend stays with us in the holidays. (often)
   _____
3   My mum and dad go out for a meal. (occasionally)
   _____

4   My sister is nice to me. (rarely)
   _____
5   My friends and I go to the cinema on a Saturday morning. (sometimes)
   _____
6   You are sad. (never)
   _____

11 ★★★ **Answer the questions so they are true for you.**

1   What do you always do at the weekend?
   _____
2   What do you rarely do after school?
   _____
3   What do you usually do when you're bored?
   _____
4   What do you sometimes do in the evening?
   _____
5   What do you never do on a Monday?
   _____
6   What do you often do when you're happy?
   _____

GET IT RIGHT!

Like + -ing

We use *like* + the *-ing* form of the verb. If the verb ends in consonant + *-e*, we drop the final *e*.
✓ *live – living*   ✗ *live – ~~liveing~~*

If a <u>short</u> verb ends in consonant + vowel + consonant, we double the final consonant before adding the *-ing*.
✓ *swim – swimming*   ✗ *swim – ~~swiming~~*

With verbs with two or more syllables, we do not usually double the final consonant.
✓ *listen – listening*   ✗ *listen – ~~listenning~~*

Correct the *-ing* forms.

1   writting   _____
2   comming   _____
3   studing   _____
4   waitting   _____
5   chating   _____
6   useing   _____
7   listenning   _____
8   planing   _____
9   rainning   _____
10 geting   _____

VOCABULARY

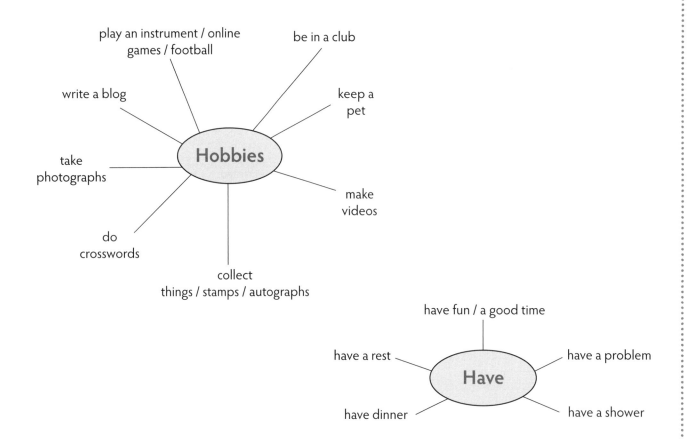

Adverbs of frequency

always   usually   often   sometimes   occasionally   rarely   never

Key words in context

have time	I never **have time** to watch TV in the morning.
have a hobby	I **have lots of hobbies** but my favourite is writing my blog.
tidy	My bedroom is very **tidy**.
busy	Sorry – I'm too **busy** to help you.
relax	My dad says that cooking the dinner helps him to **relax**.
definitely	That's **definitely** Bradley Cooper over there. I'm sure!
strange	Bird watching – that's a **strange** hobby!
smile	You never **smile** when I take your photo. You always look so sad.
positive	I feel very **positive** today. I've got a good feeling about it.
interests	My dad's got a lot of different **interests**, like reading and playing the piano.
pass the time	How do you **pass the time** when you're waiting for someone?
can't stand	Football is really, really boring. I **can't stand** it!

Hobbies `SB p.14`

1 ★☆☆ **Read the speech bubbles. Choose a word from each list and write the hobbies.**

write | collect | be | play | take | keep

a blog | an instrument | a pet | things
photographs | in a club

0

> It's about my life. It's about my friends and my families. It's about the things I enjoy doing (and some of the things I don't enjoy). It's about everything and anything. Read it!

write a blog

1

> I'm in a band. I'm the guitarist. I play for about two hours every day.

2

> We meet every Friday from 7 pm to 9 pm. We learn how to do things like how to make a fire or how to cook. It's really good fun.

3

> I've got about 50 teddy bears now. I've got big ones, medium-sized ones and small ones. Every time I visit a new city I always buy one.

4

> It's quite hard work. Every morning I wake up early to take him for a walk and then when I get home from school I take him for another walk.

5

> These are from my last holidays. We were in Corfu. It was really great. I spent hours with my camera.

2 ★★☆ **Write four words that go with each verb in the boxes.**

	a team	
an orchestra	**be in**	a club
	a band	

	collect	

	write	

	play	

3 ★★★ **Use your ideas in Exercise 2 to write four sentences that are true for you.**

I'm in the school football team.
I don't collect anything.

1 _____
2 _____
3 _____
4 _____

WordWise `SB p.19`
Collocations with *have*

4 ★★☆ **Complete the sentences. Use the words in the list.**

shower | fun | dinner | problem | rest | time

0 Do you usually have a ___*shower*___ when you wake up or before you go to bed?

1 Who do you always ask for help when you have a _____ with your homework?

2 Do you always have a _____ when you feel tired?

3 What time does your family usually have _____ ?

4 Do you always have a good _____ when you're on holiday?

5 What do you do to have _____ at the weekend?

5 ★★★ **Write answers to the questions in Exercise 4 so they are true for you.**

0 _____
1 _____
2 _____
3 _____
4 _____
5 _____

READING

1 ┃REMEMBER AND CHECK┃ **Complete the sentences with the names. Then check your answers in the blog on page 16 of the Student's Book.**

0 _Izzy_ likes spending time with an older member of her family.

1 _____ thinks she is probably different to most young people.

2 _____ loves nature.

3 _____ is interested in what's happening in the world.

4 _____ enjoys being with other people.

5 _____ is interested in finding out about new things.

6 _____ wants to meet some famous people.

7 _____ sometimes finds her hobby very relaxing.

2 **Read the text quickly. Write the names under the pictures.**

1 _____

2 _____

3 _____

Gina Jones and her sister Karen have the same hobby. They both love photography. In fact, they are both in a photography club. But they don't take photographs of their friends or the interesting places they go to. They take photographs of other people taking photographs! They have a big collection of photos – more than 2,000. They write a blog about their hobby and you can see all their photos on it. The sisters don't know the people in their photos. They are just people they see in the street. But they always ask them if they can use the photos for their blog. Most people say 'yes'.

58-year-old Dan Baker loves roller coasters. Every Saturday he visits the Alton Towers theme park and spends all day on them. Luckily he lives very near to it. Some days he has more than fifty rides. His favourites are Nemesis and Th13teen. He doesn't take his wife with him – she hates roller coasters – but he often takes his grandchildren or brother. He also collects postcards of roller coasters. Every holiday he travels to theme parks in different countries; Six Flags in Mexico, PortAventura in Spain and Everland in South Korea. But Dan wants more. He wants to ride every roller coaster in the world.

Anna Roberts is a bit different to a lot of other girls. She likes animals. That's nothing strange. Many girls her age like animals. She also keeps animals as pets. There's nothing unusual about that, either. But do most girls keep spiders, lizards and snakes? Anna does. Anna has a spider from Brazil, a lizard from Australia and a snake from South Africa. She buys them from her local pet shop. She spends all her pocket money on her pets and she also spends a lot of her time looking after them. Anna knows what she wants to do when she is older. She wants to work in the insect house at a zoo.

3 **Read the text again. Are sentences 1–5 'Right' (A) or 'Wrong' (B)? If there is**
✱ **not enough information to answer 'Right' (A) or 'Wrong' (B), choose 'Doesn't say' (C).**

0 Gina and Karen put photos of their friends on their blog.	A Right	(B) Wrong	C Doesn't say
1 Some people don't want their photos on the girls' blog.	A Right	B Wrong	C Doesn't say
2 Dan Baker is married.	A Right	B Wrong	C Doesn't say
3 Dan Baker's favourite roller coaster is in America.	A Right	B Wrong	C Doesn't say
4 Anna spends five hours every day looking after her pets.	A Right	B Wrong	C Doesn't say
5 Anna wants to look after elephants at the zoo one day.	A Right	B Wrong	C Doesn't say

DEVELOPING WRITING

Routines

1 Read about Dana's hobby. Tick (✓) the photo from her blog.

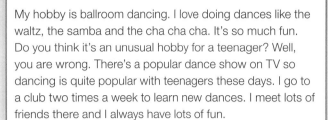

My hobby is ballroom dancing. I love doing dances like the waltz, the samba and the cha cha cha. It's so much fun. Do you think it's an unusual hobby for a teenager? Well, you are wrong. There's a popular dance show on TV so dancing is quite popular with teenagers these days. I go to a club two times a week to learn new dances. I meet lots of friends there and I always have lots of fun.

I also write a blog about dancing. It's called *Dancing with Dana*. I often take photos at the club and put them on my blog. I write something on it every day. It's a great way to meet people who have the same hobby.

2 Choose phrases from columns A, B and C to make sentences. Then check them in the text.

A	B	C
~~There's a popular dance show on TV~~	~~so~~	~~dancing is quite popular with teenagers these days.~~
I go to a club twice a week	but	learn new dances.
Maybe you think it's an unusual hobby for a teenager	and	I always have lots of fun.
I meet lots of friends there	to	you are wrong.

0 *There's a popular dance show on TV so dancing is quite popular with teenagers these days.*

1 _____

2 _____

3 _____

3 Answer the questions so they are true for you.

1 What is your hobby?

_____

2 How often do you do it?

_____

3 Where do you do it?

_____

4 Who do you do it with?

_____

5 What do you like about it?

_____

6 Is there anything you don't like about it? What?

_____

4 Use some of your ideas in Exercise 3 to complete the sentences about your hobby.

1 _____ and _____
2 _____ but _____
3 _____ so _____
4 _____ to _____

5 Write a short paragraph about your hobby (about 100–120 words). Try to use the sentences in Exercise 4.

_____

_____

_____

_____

_____

_____

_____

_____

_____

_____

_____

_____

LISTENING

1 🔊06 Listen to the conversations. Circle the correct answer A, B or C.

Conversation 1
What instrument does Danny play?

A guitar   B drums   C piano

Conversation 2
What pets has Dana got?

A a lizard   B a dog   C a lizard and a dog

Conversation 3
How many stamps has Wendy got?

A 100   B 800   C 900

DIALOGUE

1 Put the letters in order to make phrases.

1 eb / fcalure   _____

2 twahc / tou   _____

3 ntod' / od / tath   _____

2 🔊06 Use the phrases in Exercise 1 to complete the conversations. Then listen again and check.

1 Thanks, but _____. It's Alfie's guitar. It's not mine.

2 No, _____. It bites.

3 _____, Mike. Don't put your glass down there.

3 Write a short conversation for each picture. Use some of the expressions in Exercise 1.

1 _____
_____
_____
_____

2 _____
_____
_____
_____

PHRASES FOR FLUENCY   SB p.19

1 Match the words 1–6 with their meanings a–f.

1 up to   ☐
2 come on   ☐
3 look out   ☐
4 that's right   ☐
5 hurry up   ☐
6 cool   ☐

a correct

b doing

c great

d let's go

e be careful

f be quick

2 Complete the conversations with the words 1–6 from Exercise 1.

TOM   What are you ⁰ _up to_ ?

SHONA   I'm just doing a bit of drawing.

TOM   Let's have a look.

SHONA   Here. What do you think?

TOM   Is it a picture of Jen?

SHONA   ¹ _____. What do you think?

TOM   ² _____! It's really good.

LUCY   ³ _____, Ben.

BEN   OK, OK. I'm coming. Just give me a minute.

LUCY   ⁴ _____, Ben. Run.

BEN   I am running!

LUCY   ⁵ _____. Don't run into the door. Too late!

BEN   Ow! That hurts.

Reading and Writing part 3a

1 **Complete the conversations. Choose the correct answer (A, B or C).**

0 Is she Spanish?
  A Yes, she does.   (B) Yes, she is.   C Yes, she isn't.

1 Can I help you?
  A Yes, she can.   B No, I don't.   C It's OK. I'm fine.

2 Hi. I'm Alex.
  A Nice to meet you.   B Yes, you are.   C I'm happy.

3 Do you like your French teacher?
  A Yes, I like them a lot.   B Yes, I am.   C He's very good.

4 What would you like for lunch today?
  A Chicken and rice, please.   B I like fish, please.   C Yes, please.

5 Do you like dancing?
  A No, I can.   B It's OK.   C Yes, I'd love to.

Exam guide: multiple-choice replies

In the KEY Reading and Writing Part 3a you must choose the best way to reply to a statement or question. You have three possible replies to choose from.

- Read the question or statement carefully. Do you understand it? Don't look at the possible answers. How many different ways can you think of to reply? Now look at the answers. Maybe one of your ideas is there for you to choose.

- Read out the mini conversations to yourself in your head. Read the first part followed by the first possible answer. Does it sound OK? Read the first part followed by the second possible answer. Does that sound better? Read the first part followed by the third possible answer. How does that sound? If any of them don't sound right, then cross them out immediately.

- And finally – never leave a blank answer.

2 **Complete the conversations. Choose the correct answer (A, B or C).**

0 Can I ask you a question, please?
  (A) Sure, what do you want to ask?   B No, you can.   C Yes please.

1 What time do you wake up?
  A In the morning.   B About 7 am.   C After breakfast.

2 When do you do your homework?
  A Yes, I always do it.   B I usually do it after dinner.   C Sometimes.

3 How often do you go to the cinema?
  A About one time a week.   B At the weekends.   C About twice a month.

4 Have you got a tablet?
  A Yes, I have got.   B Yes, I do.   C No, I haven't.

5 Hurry up.
  A Yes, please.   B I'm OK, thanks.   C OK, I'm coming.

2 | MONEY AND HOW TO SPEND IT

GRAMMAR
Present continuous SB p.22

1 ★☆☆ Complete the sentences with the names.

0 *Sophie* and *Stella* are laughing about some crazy hats.
1 _____ is looking at the TV prices.
2 _____ is buying a digital camera.
3 _____ is trying on a T-shirt.

2 ★★☆ Complete the sentences. Use the present continuous of the verbs and the information in brackets.

0 Adrian *isn't studying English, he's studying Maths.* (– study English / + study Maths)
1 We _____, we _____.
   (+ take the bus to school / – walk)
2 Ben and Anna _____, they
   _____. (– have fun / + work on a project)
3 I _____, I _____.
   (+ try to finish my homework / – take a break)
4 We _____, we _____.
   (+ play computer games / – listen to music)
5 Abigail _____, she
   _____. (– have lunch / + help her dad)

3 ★★☆ Match the questions and answers.

0 Are you having fun?   [d]
1 Is Jim in the garden?   [ ]
2 What are you studying?   [ ]
3 Are they playing football?   [ ]
4 Am I talking too loudly?   [ ]
5 Is he studying for the test?   [ ]

a Yes, he is. He's cutting the grass.
b No, they're watching a film.
c No, don't worry. It's OK.
d No, I'm not. I've got a lot of work to do for school.
e Yes, he is. He's in his room.
f French. I'm trying to remember some new words.

4 ★★★ Complete the conversation. Use the correct form of the verbs in the list.

~~do~~ | try | not sit | sit | laugh
run | get | try | cry | laugh

LUCY   Look at that man over there! What
       0 _____ *is* _____ he _____ *doing* _____?
GAVIN Hmm. I think he 1_____ to climb the tree.
LUCY   Oh yes, there's a cat up there. Look. It
       2_____ high up in the tree.
GAVIN Oh yes. Poor cat. What's that strange noise?
       3_____ it _____
LUCY   Yeah, it's scared. Look. The man
       4_____ closer to the cat.
GAVIN But it's scared of the man too.
LUCY   Oh, no. It 5_____ to jump down. I just hope …
GAVIN There it goes. It's down.
LUCY   Wow. Look how fast it 6_____ now.
GAVIN Well, I guess it's happy it 7_____ in the tree any more.
LUCY   Hey, look at those people over there. They
       8_____ so the cat must be OK.
GAVIN That's right. And you 9_____ too now!

Pronunciation
Contractions
Go to page 118.

Verbs of perception SB p.23

5 ★★ **Look at the conversations. Circle the correct options.**

0 A What do you think of this song?
   B It *sounds* / *is sounding* really cool.
1 A What are you thinking about?
   B My homework. It *looks* / *is looking* difficult.
2 A How do you like this T-shirt?
   B It *doesn't look* / *is not looking* very nice.
3 A Would you like some cake?
   B Yes, it *smells* / *is smelling* nice.
4 A Do you like the soup?
   B Yes, it *tastes* / *is tasting* wonderful.
5 A Do you like this tattoo?
   B To be honest, I think it *looks* / *is looking* awful.

6 ★★★ **Look at the examples. Write four sentences that are true for you. Use *look*, *sound*, *smell*, *taste* and adjectives such as *interesting*, *boring*, *cool*, *awful*, *wonderful*, *exciting*.**

Raindrops on the window sound relaxing.
Lemon ice cream with chocolate chips tastes awful.

1 _____
2 _____
3 _____
4 _____

Present simple vs. present continuous
SB p.25

7 ★ **Match the pictures with the sentences.**

0 She studies English every day.   d
1 She teaches Maths.
2 She is studying for her English test.
3 She is teaching Maths.

8 ★★★ **Complete the email. Use the present continuous or the present simple of the verbs.**

Hi Ava,

I ⁰ **'m sitting** (sit) in my room in the hotel. I really ¹_____ (like) Paris. From my window I can see a park opposite the hotel. There aren't many people there. There is one woman. She ²_____ (walk) her dog. The dog ³_____ (run) after some ducks. OK, now a man ⁴_____ (try) to help her. I can't believe it! The dog has got the man's hat now, and he ⁵_____ (run) away with it. The woman ⁶_____ (shout) for the dog, but he ⁷_____ (not come) back.

How are you? What ⁸_____ (you/do)? You always ⁹_____ (play) computer games in the afternoon – ¹⁰_____ (you/do) it right now, too?

Love

Toby

GET IT RIGHT!
Present simple vs. present continuous

Present simple: for things that happen regularly or that are always true.
✓ I never **do** online shopping.
✗ I am never doing online shopping.

Present continuous: for things that are happening at or around the time of speaking.
✓ We**'re studying** English today.
✗ We study English today.

Remember: we don't usually use verbs that describe emotions or the way we think in the present continuous (e.g. *think* / *need* / *like*, etc.).
✓ I **think** it's a good idea.
✗ I'm thinking it's a good idea.

Circle the correct options.

Bike for sale!

I ¹*sell* / *am selling* my bike. It's 5 years old but it ²*is looking* / *looks* new. I ³*like* / *am liking* this bike very much, but I ⁴*want* / *am wanting* to sell it because it's too small for me.

My name is Liam and I ⁵*am coming* / *come* to school on my bike every day. I can show it to you. ☺ This week I ⁶*am studying* / *study* in room 3C. You can find me there!

VOCABULARY

It **looks** cool. It **feels** comfortable. It **sounds** nice. It **tastes** good. It **smells** awful.

chemist's newsagent's shoe shop department store

bookshop **Shops** supermarket

clothes shop post office

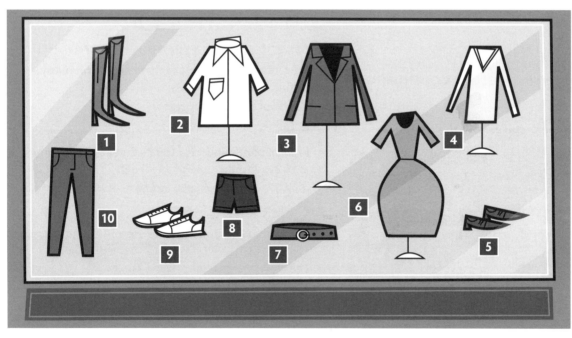

1 boots
2 shirt
3 jacket
4 jumper
5 shoes
6 dress
7 belt
8 shorts
9 trainers
10 trousers

Key words in context

customer	There aren't many **customers** in the shop right now.
size	**A** What **size** do you take?
	B Medium, please.
try on	Can I **try on** this jacket?
cost	How much does it **cost**?
spend	I don't want to **spend** so much money.
market	There are wonderful open-air **markets** in many cities.

shopping mall	Is there a **shopping mall** near here?
interested in	I'm not **interested in** designer clothes.
popular with	This shop is very **popular with** young people.
laugh at	Why are you **laughing at** me?
good-looking	Do you think he's **good-looking**?
interesting	This bookshop looks **interesting**. Let's go in.

Shops SB p.22

1 ★☆☆ Write the names of the shops under the objects.

0 _chemist's_

1 _____

2 _____

3 _____

4 _____

5 _____

2 ★★☆ Complete the conversation. Use the shops from Exercise 1.

MIA So, here's the shopping list.

LIAM OK, where do we have to go first?

MIA Let me see. Well, we need Dad's newspaper. Let's go to the ⁰_newsagent's_ first.

LIAM Wait a minute. What else do we need?

MIA Well, we need to buy stamps for this letter. The ¹_____ isn't far. Let's go.

LIAM No, no, no. I need to get jeans first. We could start at the ²_____.

MIA Don't forget. We need to get a book for Mum first. Remember – it's her birthday soon. The ³_____ closes at 5!

LIAM Absolutely, and I need some medicine for Dad. The ⁴_____ isn't too far from there.

MIA OK, and there's a ⁵_____ where we can buy all the food we need for tonight.

3 ★★★ Look at the sentences. Correct them so they are true for you.

1 There's a very good shoe shop in our town. I buy all my shoes there.

_____

2 I never go to a clothes shop. I buy all my clothes on the Internet.

_____

3 There's a newsagent's in my street. I like it.

_____

Clothes SB p.24

4 ★★☆ Write the words.

0	btle	_belt_	5	osetsrur	_____
1	tobos	_____	6	hoses	_____
2	sreds	_____	7	rtossh	_____
3	keajct	_____	8	hirst	_____
4	erpumj	_____	9	restnair	_____

5 ★★☆ Complete the text with words from Exercise 4.

Sebastian likes black. His ⁰_trousers_ and his ¹_____ are black, his ²_____ and his ³_____ are white, and he's wearing a grey ⁴_____.

6 ★★★ Write a short text about what you are wearing today.

_____

_____

_____

7 ★★☆ Match the questions and answers.

0 What do you usually wear to school? _e_

1 Do you like buying clothes? ☐

2 What's your teacher wearing today? ☐

3 Does your sister like wearing shorts? ☐

4 What do you usually wear when you're not at school? ☐

5 What do you usually wear when it's cold? ☐

a Not really. I hate shopping.

b She's wearing trousers and a jacket.

c When I'm at home, my old jumper. I love it.

d A warm coat and a hat.

e I can't choose. We all wear uniforms.

f No. She wears jeans all the time.

8 ★★★ Choose three of the questions in Exercise 7 and write answers that are true for you.

1 _____

2 _____

3 _____

READING

1 REMEMBER AND CHECK Answer the questions. Then check your answers in the script on page 21 of the Student's Book.

0 What is Tom looking for?

   A a T-shirt and some jeans   **(B)** a shirt and some trousers   **C** a T-shirt and some trousers

1 Who thinks a yellow shirt looks awful?

   A Tom   **B** Tom's parents   **C** Tom's sister

2 What does Tom think of the guy in the magazine?

   A He is very good-looking.   **B** He looks boring.   **C** His clothes are not expensive.

3 What does he think of himself?

   A He looks good in a yellow shirt.   **B** His clothes are boring.   **C** He's not good looking.

4 Who dreams of wearing fantastic clothes one day?

   A Maddy   **B** the guy in the magazine   **C** Tom

5 What does Maddy dream of?

   A ice cream   **B** being rich   **C** expensive clothes

2 Read the web chat and match the teenagers to the photos. There is no picture for one of them.

Buying or swapping – what's best?

Imagine you're looking around for clothes. You're in a really nice shop. You find a fantastic T-shirt and a cool jacket. Then you look at the prices and don't like the clothes any more. Just too expensive! Does this sometimes happen to you too? Then here's an idea for you. Maybe you should think about 'clothes swapping' – where you give clothes you don't want any more, and get others instead, at no cost!

A   **Layla, 14**

Hi, I love swapping clothes. My friends and I sometimes meet on Saturday. We all bring one piece that we don't like any more – a T-shirt, a jumper, a pair of jeans … . Then we put all the clothes on the floor. We look at them and try them on. That's a lot of fun, and we laugh a lot. Sometimes we find something we like. Then we swap. Sometimes we don't swap.

B   **Anna, 12**

I want to find something really nice at the swapping party tomorrow. A T-shirt maybe, or a jumper. My favourite colour's pink – so I'm looking for pink clothes at the moment. I've even got pink trainers, and I really like them, but they are too small for me. Maybe I can find some boots – but not in pink ;-) I often talk about clothes with my friends. I love it.

C   **William, 13**

We don't say to other boys 'I really like your T-shirt!', or 'You've got cool jeans'. I think girls say these things more often. We think it's not cool to talk about clothes. But I've got a sister, Victoria. She's 16, and she sometimes helps me, and says 'This T-shirt is nice for you' or 'Don't wear brown, it's not a good colour for you.' I like that (and my friends don't know!).

3 Read the text again. Write full sentences to answer the questions.

0 Who has got an older sister? *William has got an older sister.*

1 Who has a lot of fun swapping clothes with her friends? _____

2 Who doesn't talk to friends about clothes? _____

3 Who likes talking to friends about clothes? _____

4 Who's going to a swapping party tomorrow? _____

5 Who wants to swap a nice pair of trainers? _____

DEVELOPING WRITING

An email to say what you're doing

1   Read the emails. Who is writing on a mobile?

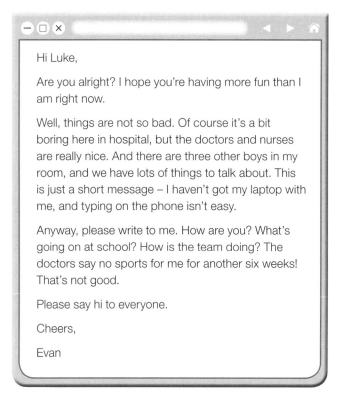

Hi Luke,

Are you alright? I hope you're having more fun than I am right now.

Well, things are not so bad. Of course it's a bit boring here in hospital, but the doctors and nurses are really nice. And there are three other boys in my room, and we have lots of things to talk about. This is just a short message – I haven't got my laptop with me, and typing on the phone isn't easy.

Anyway, please write to me. How are you? What's going on at school? How is the team doing? The doctors say no sports for me for another six weeks! That's not good.

Please say hi to everyone.

Cheers,

Evan

Hi Evelyn,

How are things with you? Hope everything's going well.

I'm with Leah and Zoe, and we're studying for the Maths test together. You know Maths is really not my favourite subject, but Leah and Zoe are really good at it. And they give me a lot of help. We're not studying right now. Leah and Zoe are playing table tennis. I'm still upstairs, but I'll join them soon.

I guess you're having a good time in London right now. You're probably walking around a street market or window shopping. Or maybe you're just buying a nice present for your sister? I'm just kidding!

By the way, we are practising for a new play at school. The first show is in two weeks' time. I hope you can come.

That's it from me. Write soon.
Lots of love,
Your sister Charlotte

2   Mark the sentences T (true) or F (false).

1   Evelyn's sister is in London now. ☐
2   Leah, Zoe and Charlotte are taking a break from studying. ☐
3   The three friends are playing a sport. ☐
4   Luke is visiting friends in hospital. ☐
5   The four boys in the hospital don't know what to talk about. ☐
6   Luke isn't happy that he can't play in the team for a long time. ☐

3   Write an informal email to a friend who is on holiday in another country (about 150 words). Use the language in the Writing tip to help you.

- Ask how your friend is.
- Tell him or her where you are and what you are doing.
- Change the subject and ask your friend a few questions about something that you are interested in.
- Say that you would like an answer as soon as possible.
- Finish with an appropriate ending.

Writing tip: informal emails

- You write informal emails to friends or family members. Your language should be informal and friendly.
- You can begin your email by asking how the other person is, for example, *How are you?, How are things with you?, Are you alright? I hope everything's well.*
- In an informal email you can use emotional expressions such as *I'm just kidding., What a pain!, How cool is that?, What a shame!*
- To change the subject, you can use phrases such as *By the way, Anyway, That reminds me of …*
- You can end your email saying what you would like the other person to do, for example, *Write soon., Let me know …, Say hi to …,* and an informal ending such as *Cheers, Love, A big hug, Talk soon,* or simply *Bye bye.*

LISTENING

1 🔊09 **Listen to the conversations and complete the sentences.**

1 The boy is interested in a ⁰ _T-shirt_ .
It's £¹_____ .
He thinks it's ²_____ .

2 The man is interested in ³_____ .
The shop assistant thinks he wants a ⁴_____ .
The book is in the section ⁵_____ the man.

3 The girl wants to see a pair of ⁶_____ .
She wants them in ⁷_____ .
She wants to ⁸_____ .

2 🔊09 **Put the conversations in order. Listen and check.**

1 BOY   OK, thanks. ☐
  BOY   Ah, OK. That's too much. ☐
  BOY   Yes. This T-shirt, how much is it? ☐
  WOMAN   Hi. Can I help you? 1
  WOMAN   Well, have a look at the T-shirts over there. They're not as pricey! ☐
  WOMAN   Let me check. Here you go … it's twenty-four pounds fifty. ☐

2 MAN   I didn't mean a recipe book. ☐
  MAN   Right. Where's that? ☐
  MAN   Hello. Have you got any books on vegetarian food? ☐
  WOMAN   Is there anything I can do for you? ☐
  WOMAN   Oh, sorry. I think you need the healthy living section. ☐
  WOMAN   Right behind you. ☐
  WOMAN   Yes, of course. That's in the section over there. There are loads of books on cooking. ☐

3 GIRL   Yes, have you got these jeans in grey? ☐
  GIRL   Thank you. Can I try them on please? ☐
  GIRL   Um … 8. ☐
  MAN   Just a moment. Here you are. ☐
  MAN   Let me look … What size do you take? ☐
  MAN   Of course. The changing rooms are over there, on your right. ☐
  MAN   Hello. Can I help? ☐

▰▰ TRAIN TO THiNK ▰▰

Exploring numbers

1 **Read the text. Can you work out how Logan finds the answer to the teacher's questions so fast? Check with the answer at the bottom of the page.**

> **Note:**
> Even numbers:
> 2 4 6 8 …
> Odd numbers:
> 1 3 5 7 …

Logan is brilliant at Maths. One day, his Maths teacher asks the class how quickly they can find the sum of the first 50 odd numbers. The other kids are starting to think when Logan calls out, '2,500'! The teacher thinks that Logan was just lucky. 'OK,' she says, 'let's make it a bit more difficult. Who's fastest at finding the sum of the first 75 odd numbers?' Everybody is thinking hard. Fifteen seconds later, Logan calls out, '5,625'! He's right again. The teacher is puzzled. How does Logan do it?

2 **A question for you: What's the sum of the first 66 odd numbers?**

_____

multiply 50 x 50, etc.
So to get the sum of the first 50 odd numbers you have to
difficult. Just multiply 9 x 9!
What's the sum of the first nine odd numbers? Again, not
multiply 3 x 3. The answer: 9!
What's the sum of the first three odd numbers? Easy! Just
numbers that start with 1. Look!
It's easy to calculate the sum of a series of consecutive odd
Answer

Listening part 1

1 🔊 **10** You will hear three short conversations. There is one question for each conversation. For each question tick (✓) A, B or C.

1   What number is Keith's house?

5   15   50

☐ A   ☐ B   ☐ C

2   What time does Tim's school start?

☐ A   ☐ B   ☐ C

3   Which picture shows what's in Dawn's bag?

☐ A   ☐ B   ☐ C

Exam guide: multiple-choice pictures

In a multiple-choice picture task, you hear short conversations and then have to choose the correct picture to answer a simple question.

- Before you listen, look at the pictures. What words do you expect to hear? These are the words you need to listen out for.
- If the pictures show numbers or times, practise saying them to yourself in your head before you listen.
- Be careful not to tick the first picture you hear. Often, you will hear all three pictures mentioned. You need to listen carefully to select the right one.
- Listen carefully to the whole conversation. The correct answer is often only revealed at the end.
- Don't worry if you don't get the answer the first time you listen. You will hear each conversation twice.
- If you get the answer on the first listening, use the second time to check the answer.
- Always choose an answer even if you have no idea which one is correct.

2 🔊 **11** You will hear five short conversations. There is one question for each conversation. For each question tick (✓) A, B or C.

1   What's the weather like?

 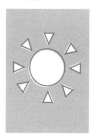 

☐ A   ☐ B   ☐ C

2   Which is Anne's dog?

☐ A   ☐ B   ☐ C

3   Where is Marco from?

Portugal   Chile   Brazil

☐ A   ☐ B   ☐ C

4   How far is Jasmine's house from her school?

☐ A   ☐ B   ☐ C

5   What is Frank's favourite sport?

☐ A   ☐ B   ☐ C

CONSOLIDATION

LISTENING

1 ◀》12 **Listen to Annie talking about her hobby. Which of these items has she got in her collection?**

2 ◀》12 **Listen again. Answer the questions.**

0 What is Annie's hobby and how is it different from other teenagers'?
She shops for clothes. It's different because she collects old clothes from the 1940s.

1 Who buys the clothes that Annie wears every day?

2 Where does Annie buy the things for her hobby?

3 Why is her collection quite small?

4 Where does she keep her collection?

5 Why doesn't she wear these clothes?

VOCABULARY

3 **Unscramble the words in *italics*.**

0 Can you go to the *rapumkerest* and get some milk?
 supermarket

1 If you're cold, then put on a *premuj*. _____

2 I'm going to the *stop cofefi* so I can get you some stamps. _____

3 Mum, I need some new *reatrins*. These have got holes in them. _____

4 The new *prentatmed toser* is really big. You can buy anything there. _____

5 Put some *hostrs* on. It's really hot today.
 _____

6 If your hands are cold, put on your *levsog*.
 _____

7 My mum's a doctor. She works at the local *sopithal*.
 _____

GRAMMAR

4 **Rewrite the sentences to include the words in brackets.**

0 I get up late on Saturday mornings. (never)
 I never get up late on Saturday mornings.

1 Dad's in the bath again. (singing)
 _____

2 That sounds a great idea. (like)
 _____

3 My dog runs after birds in the park. (always)
 _____

4 Polly like hot food but she's eating your curry. (doesn't)
 _____

5 Mum cooks at the weekend. (usually)
 _____

6 Why are you drinking the coffee? It awful. (tastes)
 _____

7 I like music but I'm enjoying listening to this! (not)
 _____

8 I go swimming on Sunday mornings. (sometimes)
 _____

9 My mum likes most fruit she doesn't like apples. (but)
 _____

10 James loves this band but he isn't the concert. (enjoying)
 _____

5 Complete the text with the present simple or present continuous form of the verbs in brackets.

Hi Archie,

I'm in Rome and I ⁰*'m having* (have) a great holiday. It's a wonderful place. At the moment I ¹_____ (sit) in a café with Jennie and I ²_____ (write) you a postcard. We ³_____ (eat) a pizza and it ⁴_____ (taste) amazing. We ⁵_____ (watch) the Italian people in the street. The people ⁶_____ (wear) really beautiful clothes here in Italy and they ⁷_____ (look) so cool. Talking of cool – all the teenagers ⁸_____ (ride) Vespas here – you know, those really great motorbikes. But they ⁹_____ (make) a lot of noise. They ¹⁰_____ (sound) like big mosquitoes.

Anyway, bye for now. The waiter ¹¹_____ (walk) over to our table with our ice cream!

DIALOGUE

6 Complete the conversation with the words in the list.

~~on~~ | problem | much | making | looks
cool | up | careful | do | right

BEN   Come ⁰___*on*___, Sue. Stop looking at the shoes.

SUE   But they're really ¹_____.

BEN   But we're here to buy George a present. Remember?

SUE   Because it's his birthday tomorrow.

BEN   That's ²_____. Now, he really likes ³_____ models so …

SUE   What about this ship?

BEN   Interesting. How ⁴_____ is it?

SUE   £200.

BEN   What! We've only got £10.

SUE   Oh. So let's forget the ship, then.

BEN   Hey, that aeroplane ⁵_____ good.

SUE   What are you ⁶_____ to, Ben?

BEN   I'm just getting this aeroplane off the shelf.

SUE   Ben – don't ⁷_____ that.

BEN   It's OK. Don't worry.

SUE   Be ⁸_____.

(CRASH!)

SUE   Oh, too late. I think we've got a ⁹_____!

READING

7 Read the text about Dan. Mark the sentences T (true) or F (false).

I've got quite an unusual hobby for a teenager. My hobby is bird watching. Some of my friends think it's a silly hobby but they don't really understand what it's all about.

I love bird watching because I get to spend a lot of time out of the house. Many teens spend most of their time indoors playing on their tablets or watching TV. I like doing that too, but not all day. I like walking in the countryside and seeing what I can find. There's always a surprise or two. I usually go bird watching at the weekend, for three or four hours in the afternoon. I sometimes go for an hour really early in the morning before school. It's the best time to see birds.

I keep a list of all the birds I see. There are more than 250 birds on it. That's most of the birds that live in the UK, but there are still a few more to see.

But the best thing about my hobby is that it doesn't cost much money. I've got a pair of binoculars – a present from my granddad – and a few books. I only need these things. Everything else is free.

0   All of Dan's friends think his hobby is great. [F]

1   Dan doesn't like playing computer games. [ ]

2   Dan always sees something different when he goes for a walk. [ ]

3   The best time to see birds is after lunch on a Saturday or Sunday. [ ]

4   Dan writes down all the birds that he sees. [ ]

5   You don't need any money to be a birdwatcher. [ ]

WRITING

8 Write a short text about your hobby (120–150 words). Include this information.

- What it is.
- When and where you do it.
- How much money you spend on it.
- Why you like doing it.

3 | FOOD FOR LIFE

GRAMMAR

Countable and uncountable nouns SB p.32

1 ★ ☆ ☆ (Circle) the correct words.

0 The books *is* / *are* on my desk.

1 The milk *is* / *are* in the kitchen.

2 There *is* / *are* three English lessons this week.

3 The cheese *is* / *are* old.

4 These apples *is* / *are* very good!

5 It *is* / *are* six o'clock.

6 My homework tonight *is* / *are* easy.

7 There *is* / *are* water on the floor.

2a ★ ☆ ☆ Write the words from Exercise 1 in the correct columns.

~~book~~ | ~~water~~ | cheese | homework
lesson | milk | time | apple

Countable	Uncountable
0 *book*	0 *water*
1	7
2	8
3	9
4	10
5	11
6	12

2b ★ ☆ ☆ Now write these words in the correct columns.

butter | computer | juice | potato | shirt | pencil

a / an / some / any SB p.32

3 ★ ☆ ☆ Complete the sentences with *a / an* or *some*.

0 I'd like ___*some*___ strawberries, please.

1 We've got _____ lesson at 10 o'clock.

2 There are _____ apples in the kitchen.

3 This is _____ old computer.

4 Let's make _____ orange juice.

5 I'd like _____ cheese sandwich, please.

6 Can I have _____ water, please?

7 You've got _____ nice shirts!

4 ★★ ☆ Complete the conversation with *some* or *any*.

DAD It's Mum's birthday tomorrow. Let's make a cake for her.

ALEX Yeah, great idea. What do we need?

DAD Well, first we need 0 ___*some*___ sugar and 1 _____ butter.

ALEX What about fruit?

DAD We're going to make a banana cake, so we need 2 _____ bananas.

ALEX OK. But we've got 3 _____ oranges and strawberries here as well. Can we use them, too?

DAD Well, maybe we can put 4 _____ strawberries on the top of the cake, but I'm sure we don't need 5 _____ oranges. It's a banana cake, Alex!

ALEX OK. Oh, it's going to be a great cake, Dad. But don't forget the candles. A birthday cake isn't right if there aren't 6 _____ candles on it.

DAD That's right.

ALEX So, can we please put 7 _____ candles on it?

DAD Sure. Now – what do we do first?

ALEX I can look on the computer to get 8 _____ information about cakes. OK?

DAD No, we haven't got 9 _____ time for that. Come on – let's start.

(how) much / (how) many / a lot of / lots of SB p.32

5 ★★★ Complete the sentences with *much* or *many*.

0 How ___*many*___ desks are there in your classroom?

1 My school hasn't got _____ computers.

2 How _____ butter do we need?

3 I haven't got _____ friends.

4 I haven't got _____ time before dinner.

5 How _____ legs has a spider got?

6 How _____ ice cream is there in the fridge?

7 We haven't got _____ homework tonight.

6 ★★☆ Replace *a lot of* with *much* or *many*.

0 I haven't got ~~a lot of~~ friends. *many*

1 There aren't a lot of people here. _____

2 There isn't a lot of sugar in my coffee. _____

3 We haven't got a lot of time. _____

4 Please don't buy a lot of cheese. _____

5 There aren't a lot of songs on this CD. _____

6 Hundreds of people went to the concert, but there weren't a lot of teenagers. _____

7 There isn't a lot of information in this book.
_____

too many / too much / not enough + noun `SB p.35`

7 ★☆☆ Complete the sentences with the words in the list.

~~too much traffic~~ | a lot of traffic | a lot of clothes
a lot of people | too many people | too many clothes

0 I can't cross the road – there's
   too much traffic!

1 I've got
   _____.
   I think I'll throw some old ones away.

2 I can't get on the bus – there are
   _____
   on it!

3 We'll get there easily – there isn't
   _____
   today!

4 I bought
   _____
   yesterday.

5 I was really happy because
   _____
   came to my party.

8 ★★☆ Circle the correct words.

0 I can't go out tonight – *I haven't got enough / I've got too much* homework to do.

1 Let's do it later. *There isn't enough / There's too much* time now.

2 We need to go shopping; *there isn't enough / there's too much* food for tonight.

3 We can't sit down because *there aren't enough / there are too many* chairs.

4 I need to tidy my room – *there aren't enough / there are too many* things on the floor!

too + adjective, (*not*) + adjective + *enough* `SB p.35`

9 ★★☆ Complete the sentences with a phrase from the list.

~~not tired enough~~ | too tired | too old
too warm | not warm enough | not old enough

0 I can't go to sleep – I'm *not tired enough*.

1 Sorry, you're only 12. You're _____ to see this film.

2 Sorry, I'm _____ to go out tonight! I just want to go to bed!

3 What? Go for a swim in the sea? Sorry, no, the water's _____.

4 I don't want to go for a walk. It's a very sunny day, so it's _____ to walk.

GET IT RIGHT!
a lot of / lots of

We use *of* + noun after *a lot* and *lots*.

✓ There are **a lot of** fast food restaurants in my town.
✗ There are ~~a lot~~ fast food restaurants in my town.
✓ We've got **lots of** money.
✗ We've got ~~lots~~ money.

We use *a* + *lot* + *of* but *lots of*.

✓ There are **a lot of** / **lots of** people at the party.
✗ There are ~~a lots of~~ people at the party.

Correct the sentences.

0 There is lots food to eat.
   There is lots of food to eat.

1 We have alot of sandwiches and a lots of sausages.
   _____

2 We don't have much of water.
   _____

3 There aren't a lot places to park the car.
   _____

4 Jo buys lots cakes and a lot ice cream.
   _____

VOCABULARY

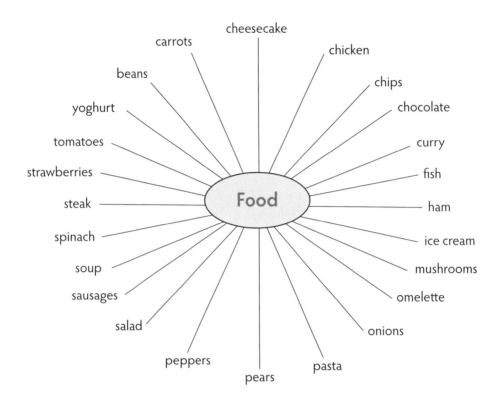

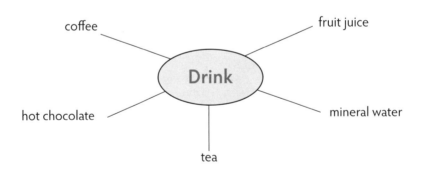

Words that go together

roast chicken
boiled potatoes
grilled fish
fried mushrooms
ham and cheese omelette
vanilla and chocolate ice cream
mixed salad
pasta with tomato sauce

Describing food

delicious
disgusting
fatty
fresh
horrible
salty
spicy
sweet
tasty
yummy

Expressions with *have got*

have got an idea
have got a headache
have got time
have got something to do
have got a problem

Food and drink [SB p.32]

1 ★☆☆ **Complete the puzzle. What is the 'mystery' word in the middle?**

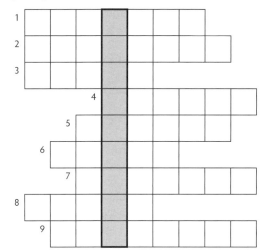

The mystery word is _____.

Adjectives to talk about food [SB p.35]

2 ★★★ Circle **the word that does not follow the adjective.**

0 roast   **a** chicken   **b** potatoes   **c** strawberries
1 grilled   **a** soup   **b** fish   **c** sausages
2 boiled   **a** carrots   **b** potatoes   **c** salad
3 fried   **a** curry   **b** chicken   **c** onions
4 mixed   **a** salad   **b** vegetables **c** chicken
5 hot   **a** water   **b** fruit juice **c** chocolate

3 ★☆☆ **Complete the adjectives. Then check in the word list 'Describing food'.**

0 de _l_ icious
1 di __ gu __ __ in __   5 s __ __ t __
2 fa __ __ y   6 s __ __ cy
3 fr __ __ h   7 s __ ee __
4 ho __ __ ib __ __   8 ta __ __ y

4 ★★☆ **Look at the words in Exercise 3. Match them to the definitions.**

0 it has a very nice taste (2 words) _delicious, tasty_
1 it has a very bad taste (2 words) _____
2 it has a lot of fat in it _____
3 it has sugar in it _____
4 it has a hot and strong taste (for example, curry)
   _____
5 it is in a natural condition (not from a tin or frozen)
   _____

5 ★★☆ **Invent two dishes, one that you think is really delicious, and one that you think is really disgusting.**

Example:

Delicious — chicken curry with mushrooms and chips
Disgusting — vanilla ice cream with spinach and chips

WordWise [SB p.37]

Expressions with *have got*

6 ★☆☆ **Match the sentences and the pictures.**

a I've got an idea!
b I've got a headache.
c I haven't got time.
d I've got something to do.

7 ★★☆ **Match the sentences to a–d in Exercise 6.**

0 'Let's go to the cinema.'   [a]
1 'I'm taking aspirin.'   [ ]
2 'And I'm going to do it now!'   [ ]
3 'Let's play tomorrow, OK?'   [ ]

READING

1 REMEMBER AND CHECK Match the statements and the food. Then check your answers in the article on page 31 of the Student's Book.

0 In Japan, they are sometimes square. [c]

1 They have more sugar in them than strawberries. ☐

2 It has a lot of vitamins that are good for the skin and hair. ☐

3 They help the body produce a chemical called 'serotonin'. ☐

4 A lot of people think they're vegetables, but they're fruit. ☐

a bananas
b avocados
c watermelons
d honey
e lemons

2 Read the text. Match the photographs and the countries.

grasshopper [1]

kudu [2]

rattlesnake [3]

chicken [4]

guinea pig [5]

chips in curry sauce [6]

a the USA
b Peru
c Brazil
d Britain
e South Africa
f Mexico

Different food around the world

It is fantastic to go to different countries. You can see wonderful places and visit great cities. You can go to museums and markets, and meet people with different ideas and a different language. And, of course, you can eat different food, too.

Sometimes the food in another country is different because it has a different taste – for example, food in India is often very spicy. But sometimes it is because the food itself is very different. So, what things do people eat in other countries that perhaps you don't eat in yours?

Well, in Mexico, some people really like to eat grasshoppers. Do you think that's strange? Perhaps, but of course the people who eat grasshoppers don't think so, and in fact grasshoppers are very good for you.

If you go to South Africa, you see that some places serve kudu – it's a kind of big antelope. And in some parts of the USA, you can eat rattlesnake – some people say it tastes like chicken, but other people say it's like fish. A lot of people just say: 'It's delicious!'

Talking of chicken, grilled chicken hearts are a big favourite in Brazil. People eat them with meat and rice at barbecues. Finally, if you go to a restaurant in some parts of Peru, it's possible that you will see fried guinea pig on the menu. It's a very important food for many people in the mountain parts of the country.

So perhaps you are thinking: 'Oh, no, please – I just want to eat chips!' Oh, yes, chips (or 'fries' in the USA). Now they're the same in every country, right? Wrong! In many places in Britain, people eat their chips with a curry sauce!

So, when you eat a meal, stop and think. Perhaps people from other countries think that your food is really strange!

3 Mark the sentences T (true) or F (false). Correct the false ones.

0 Food in India is sometimes very spicy. [T]

1 Some people eat grasshoppers in Mexico. ☐
_____

2 Grasshoppers are good for you. ☐
_____

3 Everyone thinks rattlesnake tastes like chicken. ☐
_____

4 In Brazil, some people eat fried chicken hearts. ☐
_____

5 Guinea pig is an important food everywhere in Peru. ☐
_____

6 Chips (or fries) are the same in every country. ☐
_____

7 In Britain, some people eat chips with curry sauce. ☐
_____

DEVELOPING WRITING

A recipe

1 Read the recipe for Bolognese sauce. About how long does it take to make this sauce?

frying pan

minced beef

Bolognese sauce

What you need (the ingredients):

1 tbsp olive oil
1 small carrot, cut into small pieces
1 small onion, cut into small pieces
400g can of tomatoes
some fresh basil leaves
250g minced beef
400g spaghetti
25g toasted breadcrumbs

How to make it:

1 Heat the oil in a frying pan. Put in the carrot and onion and cook for 5 minutes.

2 Add the minced beef to the carrot and onion. Cook for a few minutes (until the meat is brown).

3 Put the tomatoes into the frying pan, and cook for another 5 minutes. Stir all the time.

4 Add the basil leaves, then cook slowly for 15 minutes.

5 Cook the spaghetti. (Usually eight to ten minutes.)

6 Put the spaghetti on a plate. Put the sauce on top of the spaghetti. Put some basil leaves on top and the breadcrumbs.

2 Read the recipe again. Answer the questions.

1 How long do you cook the carrot and onion?

2 When is the meat OK?

3 How long does it take to cook the spaghetti?

4 What do you put on top of the sauce?

3 a Read the section 'How to make it' again. Match the verbs and the definitions.

1 heat ☐
2 add ☐
3 stir ☐

a put one thing together with another thing
b move round and round (often with a spoon)
c make something hot

3 b Tick (✓) the correct option.

All the verbs are in:
the present tense ☐
the imperative ☐
the past tense ☐

Writing tip: a recipe

- Choose the dish. Something simple is a good idea! (A chocolate cake? Chips? An omelette? …)
- Think of all the things you need (the ingredients). Write them down. Use a dictionary to help you with words you don't know.
- Think of any things you need to do to the ingredients before you start cooking (e.g. cut / chop / dice / …) Write the words down.
- Think of the steps ('How to make it'). What are the verbs you need? Write them down. Use a dictionary to help you with words you don't know.

4 Write a recipe for something that you know how to make or cook.

LISTENING

1 🔊 **13 Listen to the conversation between Sally and Maggie. Tick (✓) the things that Sally puts in her dish.**

beans	☐	carrots	☐
chicken	☐	chilli pepper	☐
garlic	☐	meat	☐
mushrooms	☐	onion	☐
potatoes	☐	red pepper	☐
tomato	☐		

2 🔊 **13 Listen again. Mark the sentences T (true) or F (false).**

0 Sally is cooking something for dinner. `T`

1 Sally's got an idea for a new kind of food. ☐

2 The onions, tomatoes and red peppers are grilled together. ☐

3 Sally's dish isn't spicy. ☐

4 Sally uses fried steak. ☐

5 They can eat Sally's food with salad and potatoes. ☐

6 Maggie thinks *chilli con carne* is from Mexico. ☐

7 *Chilli con carne* usually has mushrooms in it. ☐

DIALOGUE

1 Put the words in order to make phrases.

0 OK / It's. ___It's OK.___

1 sorry / I'm / really _____

2 really / I / bad / feel _____

3 it / worry / Don't / about _____

2 Use the phrases in Exercise 1 to complete the conversation. There may be more than one possible answer.

A Jacky? Do you remember that I borrowed your book?

B Yes, I remember. Why?

A Well – I can't find it. I haven't got it any more.
   0 ___I'm really sorry___.

B Oh, 1 _____, Brian. It's not a very good book!

A 2 _____, Jacky. I want to buy another one for you.

B No, Brian. 3 _____. Really. Look – I've got an idea.

A What?

B There's a film of the book now. It's at the cinema this weekend. Take me to see it!

A Oh, OK then.

PHRASES FOR FLUENCY `SB p.37`

1 Put the sentences in the correct order.

`1` A Hey, Fatima. I've got some news.

☐ A Well, they're from Italy. They're going to be here for a couple of weeks.

☐ B Oh really? What is it?

☐ A Some friends are coming next week to visit me.

☐ B So what?

☐ B Great. I love parties!

☐ A Oh, I'm sorry, Fatima, I didn't mean to. Of course I want you to come as well.

☐ B What about me? Don't forget me!

☐ B OK. Some Italians here in our town! That's good news.

☐ A Yes, it is. I want to have a party when they're here.

☐ A Me too! I'm going to invite Joe, and Garry, and June, and Melinda, and … .

2 Complete the conversations with the words in the list.

~~Actually~~ | What about me | So what
I didn't mean to | as well | a couple of

1 A Do you like this curry?
   B Yes, it's delicious. 0 ___Actually___, curry's my favourite food, I think. But I like other things 1 _____, of course.

2 A I'm going to the cinema with 2 _____ friends.
   B 3 _____? Can I come too?

3 A John's very angry with you.
   B 4 _____? I don't like him anyway.

4 A Katie? Did I say something wrong?
   B Yes. And it hurt me!
   A Well, I'm really sorry. 5 _____.

Pronunciation

Vowel sounds: /ɪ/ and /iː/
Go to page 118. 🔊

CAMBRIDGE ENGLISH: Key

Reading and Writing part 3b

1 Complete the conversation between Jack and his dad. For each space 1–5, choose one of the sentences A–H.

JACK   What's for dinner tonight, Dad?

DAD   0 _C_

JACK   Again? We had that on Monday night.

DAD   1 _____

JACK   Oh well, that's OK. I really like fish and chips. Can we have some peas too?

DAD   2 _____

JACK   Actually, they're in the cupboard, not the fridge.

DAD   3 _____

JACK   Sure. Here you are. Do you need any more help?

DAD   4 _____

JACK   Yes, it is. Is that why you cook it all the time?

DAD   5 _____

JACK   Yes, you're right. Sorry, Dad!

A   No, thanks. Cooking fish and chips is easy!

B   Can you get them for me?

C   Fish and chips.

D   We haven't got any.

E   That's not true. Sometimes I make curry.

F   I know. And we're having it again tonight.

G   I don't need any help, thanks.

H   OK. I think we've got some in the fridge.

2 Complete the conversation between a waiter and a customer. For each space 1–5, choose one of the sentences A–H.

CUSTOMER   Can I have the menu, please?

WAITER   0 _C_

CUSTOMER   Thanks. I think I'd like the mushrooms to start. Are they fresh?

WAITER   1 _____

CUSTOMER   Good, I'll have the mushrooms then.

WAITER   2 _____

CUSTOMER   The chicken, please.

WAITER   3 _____

CUSTOMER   No problem. OK, I'll have the fish, please.

WAITER   4 _____

CUSTOMER   Oh, grilled, please. And some rice and beans.

WAITER   5 _____

CUSTOMER   Just some water, please.

A   We haven't got fresh mushrooms.

B   Thank you. Would you like some water too?

C   Yes, of course. Here it is.

D   Yes, they are, Madam.

E   Of course. Would you like it grilled or fried?

F   I'm very sorry, Madam – we haven't got any chicken today.

G   Thank you, Madam. And to drink?

H   Very good, Madam. And for the main course?

Exam guide: dialogue matching

In this exercise, you read a conversation and choose a sentence to go in each of the empty spaces.

- You choose five sentences (one is given to you) from eight possibilities. This means you have to be careful not to choose sentences that are wrong.
- Remember that some of the 'wrong' answers are almost right.
- When you choose a sentence for a space, make sure it works for what is said before it, and also what is said after it. For example, look at space number 2 above. Jack says: 'Can we have some peas too?' A possible answer is D: 'We haven't got any.' BUT – and this is important – Jack then says: 'Actually, they're in the cupboard … '. So D cannot be correct. The correct answer is H. (Another example: why is 'G' NOT the right answer for space 4?)
- When you finish choosing the sentences, read through the complete conversation again to check your answers. Does the conversation make sense?

GRAMMAR
Possessive adjectives and pronouns
`SB p.40`

1 ★ ☆ ☆ (Circle) the correct words.

⁰I / *My* family is quite big. There are ¹I / *my* three sisters Vicky, Mila and Madison, and there are ²*us* / *our* brothers Dylan and Isaac. And ³I / *my* name's Ryan, so we are three boys and three girls. ⁴*Us* / *Our* sisters love playing football for the school team. ⁵*They* / *Their* team is really good. Vicky is ⁶*they* / *their* goalkeeper. ⁷*She* / *Her* friends think she's the best goalkeeper in the world. ⁸*Us* / *Our* mum and dad love football too, so on Sundays we all go and watch the three girls play. Dad's got a brother. ⁹*He* / *His* name's Jonathan. He sometimes goes with us to watch the girls play. Uncle Jonathan often says to me, ¹⁰'*You* / *Your* sisters are good footballers, but I'm sure you are better.' I think that's funny.

2 ★★☆ Rewrite the sentences using possessive pronouns.

0 Is this your dog? *Is this dog yours?*

1 Is that his car? _____

2 Are these your jeans? _____

3 Is this my sandwich? _____

4 Are these our books? _____

5 Is that her house? _____

Whose and possessive *'s*   `SB p.40`

3 ★ ☆ ☆ Look at the example. Write sentences in the same style. In each sentence, put the apostrophe in the right position.

0 A Whose is this pen?
   B It's his. (Peter) *I think it's Peter's.*

1 A Whose are those shoes?
   B They're theirs. (my friends) _____

2 A Is this your car?
   B No, it's hers. (Mrs Miller) _____

3 A Are those your brothers' bikes?
   B No, they're theirs. (my sisters) _____

4 A Is this John's phone?
   B No, it's his. (Tom) _____

5 A Whose are these keys?
   B They're hers. (Sandra) _____

4 ★★ ☆ (Circle) the correct words.

0 A Can you check (who's) / *whose* at the door?
   B It's (Peter's) / *Peter* friend, Henry.

1 A *Who's* / *Whose* car is this?
   B It's the *Miller's* / *Millers'* new car.

2 A Is it *Sam* / *Sam's* bike?
   B No, it's his sister *Barbara* / *Barbara's*.

3 A Our *teacher's* / *teachers* son is a doctor.
   B You mean Mrs *Smith's* / *Smith* son?

4 A *Who's* / *Whose* your favourite band?
   B I really like The Arctic *Monkey's* / *Monkeys'* songs a lot.

5 A *Who's* / *Whose* are these books?
   B They aren't mine. I think they're *James* / *James's*.

5 ★★★ Complete the conversations.

1 A I really like ⁰ *your* jacket, Bob. It looks really good on ¹_____.
   B ²_____ isn't ³_____. It's Kev's. He lent it to ⁴_____. I've got to give it back to ⁵_____ later.

2 A Do you know the Richard twins? ⁶_____ live next to Sally. In fact she lives at number 9, and ⁷_____ house is number 11.
   B Yes, I know Sally. My sister is a good friend of ⁸_____. She's a friend of mine too.

3 A I'm sure that's Liam's dog over there. So where is ⁹_____? He never goes anywhere without ¹⁰_____ dog.
   B It's not ¹¹_____. Liam's dog is black and that one is brown.

4 A Hey, what are ¹²_____ doing, Henry? That's ¹³_____ sandwich. It's not ¹⁴_____!
   B I'm sorry. ¹⁵_____ was hungry. Here ¹⁶_____ are. Don't be angry with ¹⁷_____, OK?

5 A ¹⁸_____ is this camera?
   B Let's ask Joseph. I think it's ¹⁹_____. Or talk to Rebecca. Maybe it's ²⁰_____.

Pronunciation
-er /ə/ at the end of words
Go to page 119.

was / were   SB p.43

6 ★☆☆ (Circle) the correct option.

0   Breakfast this morning (was) / were delicious, but the bananas wasn't / (weren't) very sweet.

1   Mrs Donald, our English teacher, was / were really cool yesterday. We was / were happy too.

2   My parents wasn't / weren't at home yesterday evening. They was / were at my school with my teacher.

3   I was / were really hungry but there wasn't / weren't any sandwiches left.

4   The film was / were really boring. We wasn't / weren't very interested in it.

5   They was / were very late. There wasn't / weren't many people left at the party.

7 ★☆☆ Complete the sentences with was or were.

0   A   _Was_ it cold this morning?
    B   Cold? Not really.

1   A   _____ David and Daniel born in the same year?
    B   No. David is 9, Daniel is 11.

2   A   _____ your parents angry with you?
    B   Not at all.

3   A   _____ all your friends at your party?
    B   Only Tony wasn't. He was ill.

4   A   _____ she hungry?
    B   Yes, very, very hungry.

5   A   _____ they at home?
    B   No, they _____ still at school.

8 ★★☆ Complete the dialogue between a police officer (PO) and Eric with was, wasn't, were or weren't.

PO   So, just let me check your story again.
ERIC   Sure.
PO   Your mum and dad ⁰ _were_ in the garden.
ERIC   Yes, they ¹_____. They ²_____ very happy.
PO   And your brother ³_____ in the garden too.
ERIC   No, he ⁴_____. He ⁵_____ in the garage. He ⁶_____ very happy. In fact, he ⁷_____ very angry.
PO   And ⁸_____ your sister, Jill, in the house?

ERIC   Yes, she ⁹_____. She ¹⁰_____ in the kitchen. She ¹¹_____ very hungry.
PO   And the twins? ¹²_____ they in the kitchen with her?
ERIC   No, they ¹³_____. They ¹⁴_____ in the living room – in front of the TV.
PO   And you, Eric. Where ¹⁵_____ you?
ERIC   I ¹⁶_____ tired and I ¹⁷_____ very well. I ¹⁸_____ in bed.
PO   Sleeping.
ERIC   Yes, I ¹⁹_____ asleep.
PO   So, if you ²⁰_____ asleep, how do you know where everyone was?

9 ★★☆ Answer the questions so they are true for you.

1   Were you at school yesterday at 3 pm?
    _____

2   Was it hot yesterday?
    _____

3   Was your teacher happy this morning?
    _____

4   Were you in bed early last night?
    _____

5   Were you late to school last week?
    _____

6   Was your best friend happy to see you this morning?
    _____

GET IT RIGHT!

it's and its

We use **it's** as a short form of **it is**. We always use an apostrophe (') between **it** and the **-s**.

✓ *It's my mum's birthday today.*
✗ *I̶t̶s̶ my mum's birthday today.*

We use **its** to talk about possession when the subject is an object or an animal*. **Its** never has an apostrophe.

✓ *This book's very old. **Its** pages are yellow.*
✗ *This book's very old. I̶t̶'s̶ ̶p̶a̶g̶e̶s̶ are yellow.*

*We sometimes use **his/her** to talk about animals that are our pets.

Put four apostrophes (') in the correct place.

I love my new mobile phone. I love the colour. Its red. Its my favourite colour. The screen is big and the camera takes good pictures. My sister loves her phone because of its modern design and its apps and because its small. Her friends gave it to her for her birthday. Its really nice, but I think mine is the best.

VOCABULARY

Family members

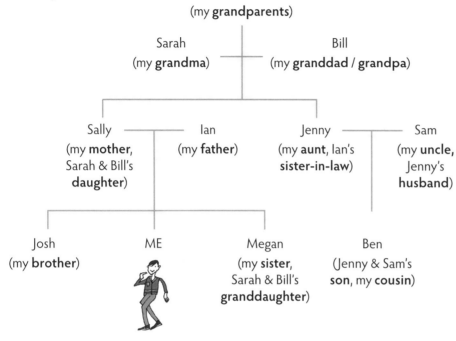

(my **grandparents**)

Sarah
(my **grandma**)

Bill
(my **granddad / grandpa**)

Sally
(my **mother**,
Sarah & Bill's
daughter)

Ian
(my **father**)

Jenny
(my **aunt**, Ian's
sister-in-law)

Sam
(my **uncle**,
Jenny's
husband)

Josh
(my **brother**)

ME

Megan
(my **sister**,
Sarah & Bill's
granddaughter)

Ben
(Jenny & Sam's
son, my **cousin**)

Possessive adjectives and pronouns

Possessive adjectives	Possessive pronouns
my	mine
your	yours
his	his
her	hers
its	–
our	ours
their	theirs

Key words in context

side of the family	Here's a photo of my dad's **side of the family**.
fight	They are three brothers and they **fight** quite a lot.
spend time	Do you **spend** a lot of **time** with your family?
hero	Miya and Tiffany are **heroes** – they saved their father's life.
ambulance	Let's call the **ambulance**. Quick!
disappear	David **disappears** under the water.
in trouble	I think they're **in trouble**. Let's help them.
open presents	Can we **open** our **presents** now?
watch a performance	Let's **watch the 6 pm performance**.
international	When is **International** Children's Day?
national	Today is a **national** holiday in Turkey.
share	Let's **share** the pizza. It's big enough.
together	It's good for children and parents to have time to spend **together**.
invitation	Thanks for the **invitation** to the party.

Feelings

upset

angry

surprised

confused

proud

relieved

worried

scared

Family members `SB p.40`

1 ★★☆ **Do the crossword. Find the famous father of Maddox, Pax, Zahara, Shiloh, Knox and Vivienne in the shaded squares.**

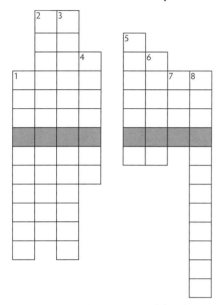

1 My parent's son. He's older than me.
2 He's married to my sister.
3 My son's daughter.
4 My dad's mum.
5 My mum's dad.
6 The son or daughter of my uncle.
7 My mum's sister.
8 My parent's daughter. She's younger than me.

2 ★★★ **Look at the example. Think of famous people or other people you know and write sentences about them.**

0 a little brother
Prince Harry is Prince William's younger brother.

1 a big sister

2 a father-in-law

3 cousins

4 a grandpa

5 an uncle

6 a sister-in-law

7 an aunt

Feelings `SB p.43`

3 ★★☆ **Unscramble the words in the list. Write them under the pictures.**

~~purerissd~~ | cusdefno | droup | drewori
deliever | credas | estup | grany

0 *surprised*   1

2   3

4   5

6   7

4 ★★☆ **How do you feel when …**

0 you watch a horror film?
I feel scared!

1 you get bottom marks in a test?

2 you get top marks in a test?

3 you don't understand a lesson?

4 your best friend forgets your birthday?

5 you've got an important test in the morning?

6 a test is over (and it wasn't so difficult)?

7 your grandparents give you some money (and it's not even your birthday)?

READING

1 REMEMBER AND CHECK **Complete the sentences. Then check your answers in the article on page 39 of the Student's Book.**

0 Marge Simpson is Homer's _wife_ .

1 Homer is Lisa and Maggie's _____

2 Ben's on _____ with his Grandpa and Gwen.

3 Ben and Gwen, the two _____, fight quite a lot.

4 Greg is the middle _____ of the Heffley family.

5 He is Roderick's _____ brother.

2 Read the TV guide quickly. What relationship is …

1 Joe to Lucy?_____

2 John to Paul?_____

3 Read the TV guide again. Are sentences 1–7 'Right' (A) or 'Wrong' (B)? If there isn't enough information to answer 'Right' or 'Wrong', choose 'Doesn't say' (C).

0 *We're Watching You* is on twice a week.

  A Right   B Wrong   Ⓒ Doesn't say

1 There are famous actors in the show.

  A Right   B Wrong   C Doesn't say

2 The show makes the reviewer laugh.

  A Right   B Wrong   C Doesn't say

3 The families behave badly for the camera.

  A Right   B Wrong   C Doesn't say

4 No-one in the Collins family is happy with what they watch.

  A Right   B Wrong   C Doesn't say

5 Anna Collins is good at sport.

  A Right   B Wrong   C Doesn't say

6 The Lawson family like action films.

  A Right   B Wrong   C Doesn't say

7 Saturday nights don't usually have a happy ending for the Lawsons.

  A Right   B Wrong   C Doesn't say

4 Answer the questions.

0 Why do people like watching the show?

  It's really funny.

1 What does Joe and Lucy's dad like watching?

_____

2 What does Joe's sister want?

_____

3 Whose grandpa can't hear very well?

_____

4 What does John's grandson want to do?

_____

TV Guide: *We're Watching You*

Watching TV families watching TV

We're Watching You is a simple but brilliant idea; put a tiny camera on the front of the TVs in several family homes and record them, and then make it into a TV programme. And that's all it is, a TV programme that shows us real people watching real TV. Exciting? Not really. But it is really, really funny.

Of course, all the people on the show agree to the camera being on their TV but they soon forget it's there and then the problems start.

There are the Collins family from Huddersfield. Mike, the dad, can never find the remote control, and soon starts shouting at his kids, Joe and Lucy, to find it. Of course, as his wife Anna says, he always finds it – he usually sits on it. Anna only wants to watch sport, her husband wants cooking programmes, Joe wants cartoons and Lucy wants a quiet house without TV. No-one usually gets what they want.

And then there's the Lawson family from Taunton. They sit down together and watch a film every Saturday night. It always starts off well but soon there's action. Grandpa John can't hear very well. He always wants to turn the volume up. This upsets his daughter, Georgia, who hates the loud noise. So Grandpa turns it down, but then he asks his grandson, Paul, to tell him what people say. This makes Paul angry. And then his mum often walks in front of the TV into the kitchen to get a cup of tea. Poor Paul – he doesn't want a cup of tea, he just wants to watch the film.

We're Watching You is fun to watch but I'm glad these cameras aren't in my home!

DEVELOPING WRITING

An invitation

1 Read the invitations. Put the events in the order that they start on Friday.

1	The sleepover
	The film
	The school show
	The party

A

Hayden,

Can you come to my birthday party at The Fun Factory? It's on Friday evening from 6 pm to 10 pm. They do food there so don't eat before! Please let me know if you can come so I can tell the organisers how many people to expect. Hope you can come.

Best,

Don

B

Joe,

Do you want to go to the cinema on Friday to see the new Bond film? There's a show at 7 pm so we can meet at 6 pm and have a pizza at the café, if you'd like. Let me know if you can come.

Ian

C

Dear Aunt Beth,

There's a show on at my school next Friday and I'm in it. I'd love it if you could come. It starts at 6.30 pm but get there early if you want a good seat. The school's at the beginning of Brook Lane. There's a lot of space to park. Hope to see you there.

Dawn

D

Dear Jasmine,

Would you like to come to a sleepover at my house this Friday? We can come and pick you up at about 5 pm and take you back on Saturday afternoon. Please say 'yes'. We'll have fun.

Susie

PS My mum says you have to ask your parents first.

2 Look at the lines from the replies. Match them with the invitations.

0 Mum and Dad want me back before lunch if that's OK. **D**

1 By the way, what do you want for a present?

2 I can be there at 6 pm. I want a seat right in the front row!

3 Sorry, I can't be there at that time. I'd love to see it. Is there a later show – around 8 pm?

Writing tip: An invitation

If you want someone to do something with you, you might send them an invitation.

- Invitations don't need to be long but they do need to contain all the important information – what the event is, where it is, what time it starts, etc.
- If you know the person well you might not need to include information such as where you live or your telephone number. So think carefully about what the important information is.
- If the invitation is to a friend, use more informal language and make your invitation sound friendly. Remember, you want this person to say 'yes'. Use expressions to make them feel very welcome; *please come, I hope you can come, please say 'yes'*, etc.
- More formal invitations need more formal language. Address the person with *Dear* and use expressions like *Would you like to come … ?* rather than *Do you want to … ?*
- Don't forget to ask for a reply.

3 Write an invitation (50–60 words). Choose one of these reasons.

1 You want your teacher to come and watch your band play on Friday evening.

2 You want your best friend to play tennis after school.

3 You want your friend to go away with you and your family for the weekend.

_____
_____
_____
_____
_____
_____

LISTENING

1 🔊 17 Listen to the conversations. Put the pictures in order.

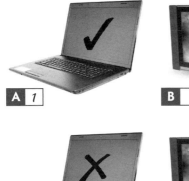

A 1

B

C

D

2 🔊 17 Listen again. Mark the statements T (true) or F (false).

0   In conversation 1 the girl wants to do her homework. [T]

1   The girl can borrow her mum's laptop. ☐

2   In conversation 2 the girl can't borrow her mum's laptop. ☐

3   In conversation 3 the boy wants to play a video game. ☐

4   He says his homework is for Thursday. ☐

5   In conversation 4 the father gives the boy the remote control. ☐

3 Put the words in the correct order to make conversations.

1   A   I / laptop / Can / borrow / your?

0   *Can I borrow your laptop?*

    B   Why / to / you / borrow / do / it / want?

1   _____

    A   want / I / homework / to / do / my.

2   _____

    B   can / course / OK, / you / of.

3   _____

2   A   we / TV / Can / watch / some?

4   _____

    B   homework / you / Have / any / got?

5   _____

    A   Friday / it's / Yes / only / but / for.

6   _____

    B   you / no / can't / Well. your / Do / first / homework.

7   _____

DIALOGUE

1 Write a conversation for each of these pictures Use a request in each conversation, with a positive answer in one, and a negative answer in the other.

TOM   _____

ALAN _____

TOM   _____

ALAN _____

SALLY _____

MUM   _____

SALLY _____

MUM   _____

▶ TRAIN TO THiNK ◀

Making inferences

1 Look at the text on page 40 of the Workbook again. Who do you think says these things? Choose from the names in the list.

John | Georgia | Paul | Mike | Joe | Anna | Lucy

0   What did he say? *John*

1   It's my turn and we're watching football. _____

2   Can't we just turn it off! _____

3   Shh! They're giving us a really good recipe for a cake. _____

4   Why don't you look under your legs? _____

5   No, Mum, I don't want anything to eat, thank you!
    _____

6   Where is it? I want to change channel. _____

7   Can you turn it up a bit? _____

8   Not tennis again. I want to watch *Batman*.
    _____

9   Please – turn it down! _____

CAMBRIDGE ENGLISH: Key

Reading and Writing part 6

1 **Read the descriptions of family members. Complete the words.**

0   My mum's mum   g r a n d m a

1   My mum's dad   g _ _ _ _ _ _

2   My mum's sister   a _ _ _

3   My mum's brother   u _ _ _ _

4   The children of 2 or 3 above

    c _ _ _ _ _ _

Exam guide: word completion

In the word completion activity you read five definitions and you have to write the word. You are given the first letter.

- In this activity it's important that your spelling is correct, so it's a good idea to write the words on a piece of paper before you write on the answer sheet.
- Make sure your answers have the right number of letters – there is one letter for each gap.
- Always read the instructions carefully – they tell you what category of words you have to think of (e.g. 'family members').
- Always learn words in groups, as you can find them on the third page of every unit in this Workbook. This helps you to remember words better.

2 **Read the descriptions of feelings. Complete the words.**

0   When you aren't happy   u p s e t

1   When you really don't know what to do

    c _ _ _ _ _ _ _

2   When you don't expect something

    s _ _ _ _ _ _ _ _

3   When you are a bit nervous about something

    w _ _ _ _ _ _

4   When you are happy because a bad thing is over

    r _ _ _ _ _ _ _

Listening part 3

1 🔊 **18** **Listen to Olivia talking to Dave about her family. For each question, choose the right answer A, B or C.**

0   Beth's husband is …

  A French.   B Scottish.   C Irish.

1   Olivia has got …

  A one sister.   B two sisters.   C three sisters.

2   Luke is …

  A 8 weeks old.   B 8 months old.   C 8 years old.

3   Olivia's grandpa is called …

  A William.   B Tony.   C Roger.

4   Dave thinks Olivia looks like her …

  A cousin.   B mother.   C father.

Exam guide: multiple-choice listening

In the multiple-choice listening question, you will hear a conversation between two people. You have to choose the correct option to complete sentences about the conversation.

- Before you listen, read through all the questions. This will tell you what the listening is about.
- Look at each question carefully and identify the kind of information you need to listen out for.
- The questions come in the same order that they are in the listening. This will help you not to get lost while you listen.
- Don't worry if you miss the answer to one question. Just move on to the next one.
- You'll hear the conversation twice. Use the second time to listen for missing answers and check the answers you already have.
- Finally, don't leave an answer blank. Always have a guess.

2 🔊 **19** **Listen to Liam talking to Rachel about a new restaurant. For each question, choose the right answer A, B or C.**

0   The new restaurant is …

  A French.   B Italian.   C Mexican.

1   The restaurant is in …

  A High Street.   B River Street.   C Bridge Street.

2   Rachel was there last …

  A Friday.   B Wednesday.   C weekend.

3   Her meal was …

  A £9.   B £9.50.   C £10.

4   Rachel was there …

  A with her family.   B in the afternoon.   C for her birthday.

CONSOLIDATION

LISTENING

1 🔊**20** **Listen to the conversation. Circle A, B or C.**

1 What does the man want to drink?

   A orange juice   **B** water with ice and lemon   **C** water

2 What does the young woman want to drink?

   A mineral water   **B** tea   **C** lemonade

3 What soup would the man like to have?

   A mushroom   **B** chicken   **C** tomato

2 🔊**20** **Listen again. Answer the questions.**

0 Why does the man order mineral water?

   Because there isn't any orange juice.

1 What does the waitress bring the man?

2 Whose is the drink?

3 In the third conversation what does the man want to eat?

4 What does he think about the place?

5 Where does he arrange to meet Lisa?

GRAMMAR

3 **Circle the correct word.**

1 **A** Is that your book?

   B No, it's *her / hers*.

2 **A** Is that your grandpa's watch?

   B Yes, it's *his / hers*.

3 **A** Have you got a cat?

   B Yes, I have. *It's / Its* name is Tigger.

4 **A** Do you like your new phone?

   B Yes, I do and *it's / its* got a really good camera too.

5 **A** *Whose / Who's* are those trainers?

   B They're mine.

4 **Circle the correct words.**

NATALIE ⁰*Was / Were* you at the cinema with Joan and Lucas last night?

JOSEPH Yes, I ¹*was / were*. It ²*was / were* a lot of fun.

NATALIE And then? ³*Was / Were* you all at the fast food place again?

JOSEPH How do you know? We ⁴*was / were*, actually.

NATALIE Oh, I also know what you had. You always have ⁵*some / any* sausages, ⁶*a lot of / much* chips, and you don't eat ⁷*some / any* vegetables.

JOSEPH Yeah, I know. I don't eat ⁸*too much / enough* healthy food, you're right.

NATALIE Hey, I've got an idea. Come and have lunch at our place. My dad's a good cook. He's a vegetarian so he doesn't cook ⁹*some / any* meat but he makes ¹⁰*much / lots of* excellent salads.

JOSEPH Thanks, that sounds good.

NATALIE Well, come tomorrow at 12.30.

JOSEPH Great, thanks.

VOCABULARY

5 **Unscramble the adjectives in brackets. Complete the sentences.**

0 How would you like your vegetables, *boiled* (deilob) or *grilled* (llrigde)?

1 This curry is too _____ (ypisc) for me, I'm afraid.

2 I'm sorry, but this smells so _____ (unstsdgiig) that I can't eat it.

3 **A** Do you think the soup's too _____ (aslyt)?

   B No, not at all. I think it's very _____ (yttas).

4 This steak is nice, and the salad's _____ (cidesliou).

5 **A** How do you like the _____ (staro) chicken?

   B It's absolutely _____ (uymym).

6 These vegetables are all really _____ (hefrs).

7 This cheesecake's just not very good. It's too _____ (weset), and it tastes a bit _____ (igorbn).

6 Complete the sentences. Use words for family members and feelings. Use the ideas in brackets and the first letters to help you.

0   It's my *little sister's* (I'm her big brother) birthday next week. She doesn't know that I'm organising a party. She'll be very *surprised* when she finds out.

1   My _____ (mother's father) loves taking photos. He's always p_____ when he can show them to us.

2   My _____ (uncle's wife) was in hospital for a few days. We're all r_____ she's OK again.

3   My _____ (uncle's daughter) Joanna hates horror films. They make her really s_____.

4   Roy and Christina are _____ and wife (married). They are u_____ because their daughter Caroline never visits them.

DIALOGUE

7 Complete the conversation. Use the phrases in the list.

~~can I borrow~~ | feel really bad | what about
didn't mean to | can I, please | a couple of
I'm so sorry | don't worry | of course | that's OK

ZOE   Jordan, ⁰ *can I borrow* your MP3 player?

JORDAN   ¹_____ you can. Your big brother never says 'no', does he?

ZOE   That's right. Thanks so much. Bye.

JORDAN   Where are you going?

ZOE   I'm going to meet Mia and Emily.

JORDAN   And ²_____ my MP3 player? Are you taking it with you?

ZOE   ³_____? It's only ⁴_____ hours. I'll be back soon.

JORDAN   ⁵_____. But make sure you bring it back.

(later)

JORDAN   Ah, you're back.

ZOE   Well, yes, but I ⁶_____. The MP3 player. It's broken.

JORDAN   I can't believe it.

ZOE   ⁷_____, Jordan. I ⁸_____ break it. It was an accident.

JORDAN   OK, ⁹_____. These things happen. But next time … Your big brother will say 'no'!

READING

8 Read the magazine article about unusual birthday traditions. Mark the sentences T (true) or F (false).

Happy birthday – the world over

HOW do you celebrate your birthday? With a cake, a party for your friends, with games and fun for all? In some countries birthday celebrations are really unusual.

In some parts of India, for example, when a child has their first birthday, their parents cut off all their hair. The birthday child wears colourful clothes and gives chocolate to all their friends.

In Vietnam, they celebrate everybody's birthday on New Year's Eve. Parents give their children a paper envelope with coins in it – 'lucky money'.

In Korea, they celebrate day number 100 after the child is born. Children get rice cakes with honey and red and black beans. Families make sure a child gets a lot of these rice cakes. When a child gets a hundred rice cakes this means that they will live a happy and long life.

When children in Denmark wake up on their birthday, there are presents all around the bed on the floor. That's why some of the children are so excited that they find it difficult to fall asleep the night before!

0   In India children get chocolate from their friends on their birthdays. [F]

1   Parents in some parts of India cut off their children's hair on their first birthdays. [ ]

2   In Vietnam they only celebrate children's birthdays on the last day of the year. [ ]

3   In Korea they celebrate before a child is four months old. [ ]

4   Children in Korea get lots of rice cakes with chocolate and ice cream. [ ]

5   In Denmark children get their presents the night before their birthdays. [ ]

WRITING

9 Write a paragraph about how you celebrate your birthday (about 80–100 words). Use the questions to help you.

- How important are birthdays in your family?
- How do you celebrate them?
- Are there any interesting traditions?

5 | IT FEELS LIKE HOME

GRAMMAR
Past simple (regular verbs) SB p.50

1 ★ ☆ ☆ **Find nine more verbs in the word search and write them next to the past forms.**

S	T	A	Y	D	U	T	S	T	W	L
T	W	T	R	E	V	I	R	R	A	P
O	R	M	D	V	E	S	U	T	N	A
P	L	A	N	K	L	I	K	E	T	S
L	I	R	E	R	R	V	A	R	N	W

0	_stay_	stayed	5	_____	studied
1	_____	liked	6	_____	wanted
2	_____	arrived	7	_____	visited
3	_____	planned	8	_____	stopped
4	_____	dried	9	_____	used

2 ★★ ☆ **Use the past tenses in Exercise 1 to complete the sentences.**

0 The bus _arrived_ thirty minutes late.
1 We _____ to go to the beach.
2 The test was really important so I _____ all weekend for it.
3 I really _____ the film. It was so funny.
4 We _____ my uncle in Spain for our holidays.
5 We _____ in a really expensive hotel on our last holidays. It was great.
6 She _____ playing football because of an accident.
7 I _____ my birthday party very carefully. I wanted it to be perfect.
8 My hair was wet so I _____ it with your towel.

3 ★★ ☆ **Write the past forms of the verbs.**

0	call	_called_	6	love	_____
1	start	_____	7	ask	_____
2	try	_____	8	finish	_____
3	seem	_____	9	look	_____
4	watch	_____	10	show	_____
5	enjoy	_____	11	decide	_____

4 ★★★ **Complete the story with the past forms of the verbs in brackets.**

When I was younger I [0] _loved_ (love) LEGO. My sister and I [1] _____ (play) with it all the time. I always [2] _____ (ask) for LEGO for my birthday. I was a member of the LEGO Club. Every three months a magazine [3] _____ (arrive) in the post. It was full of ideas for models you could build and there were photos of models from club members. Each time I [4] _____ (open) the magazine, I [5] _____ (look) at that page for hours. I [6] _____ (dream) of seeing one of my models on that page. One day my sister and I [7] _____ (decide) to build the best model ever and send a photo to the magazine. For days we [8] _____ (work) on it. We [9] _____ (use) so many different types of bricks, big ones, small ones, square ones, round ones, red ones, blues one – every shape and colour you can imagine. After about a week we [10] _____ (finish). It was amazing and we were so happy. Then we [11] _____ (need) to take a photo of it. Very carefully I [12] _____ (pick) it up and [13] _____ (carry) it down the stairs. My sister [14] _____ (open) the kitchen door and there were three more steps to the kitchen table. Unfortunately, the dog was sitting between me and the table. He [15] _____ (jump) up and [16] _____ (knock) the model to the floor. It [17] _____ (smash) into thousands of pieces. We [18] _____ (try) to fix it but it was useless. I [19] _____ (look) at my sister and we both [20] _____ (realise) it was the end of our dream.

Pronunciation
Regular past tense endings
Go to page 119.

Modifiers: *quite, very, really* `SB p.51`

5 ★★ **Write sentences with the words in brackets.**

0 I'm not happy today. (very)
   I'm not very happy today.

1 Your grandmother is young. (really)
   _____

2 Hurry up. We're late. (very)
   _____

3 Can I have a sandwich? I'm hungry. (quite)
   _____

4 I'm tired. I want to go to bed. (quite)
   _____

6 ★★ (Circle) **the best word.**

0 It's 40°C today. It's *quite /* (really) hot!

1 That song's OK. It's *quite / very* good.

2 This bed is so uncomfortable. It's *quite / very* hard.

3 The sea's *quite / very* cold today. Don't go in it. You'll freeze!

4 That food is *quite / really* delicious. I want to eat it all.

Past simple negative `SB p.53`

7 ★ **Match the sentence halves.**

0 I chatted to her for an hour — `c`
1 He downloaded the game — ☐
2 She posted the card on Monday — ☐
3 He cooked them a really special meal — ☐
4 The team played really well — ☐

a but it didn't arrive for my birthday.
b but we didn't win.
c but we didn't talk about you.
d but they didn't really like it.
e but it didn't work.

8 ★★ **Make the sentences negative.**

0 I liked the ice cream.
   I didn't like the ice cream.

1 We enjoyed the film.
   _____

2 They went to France for their holidays.
   _____

3 She wanted to go to the party.
   _____

4 He won 1st prize in the photography competition.
   _____

5 You met Dan at my party.
   _____

9 ★★ **Complete Jenny's holiday blog with the correct form of the words in the list.**

not like | not look | ~~arrive~~ | not think
stop | not work | not want | want

Day 8 Ice cream in Rome

We ^{0} _arrived_ in Rome last night at about 7 pm. Dad really wanted to see the Trevi fountain. I ^{1}_____ to see it. I wanted to watch some TV and get an early night. But Dad is the boss and so we all followed him there. Then Dad asked me to take a photo of him by the fountain. He ^{2}_____ very cool in his silly hat so I refused. He ^{3}_____ that very much. On our way back to the hotel we ^{4}_____ to buy some ice cream. I didn't want to stop. I just ^{5}_____ to get to bed. But Dad, as I already said, is the boss so we stopped. Well, this time I was wrong. What a fantastic ice cream. It was delicious. The best ice cream ever. I ^{6}_____ an ice cream could taste so good! Anyway, we arrived back in the hotel about 10 pm. I tried to watch some TV but it ^{7}_____ so I just went to bed and dreamed about ice cream all night.

GET IT RIGHT! ⊙
Past simple (regular verbs)

We add *-ed* to verbs ending in vowel + *-y* (e.g. *played*).
✓ play – played
✗ play – ~~plaid~~

If the verb ends in consonant + *-y* (e.g. *try*), we change the *-y* to *-i* and add *-ed*.
✓ try – tried
✗ try – ~~tryed~~

Correct the past simple forms.

1 plaid _____
2 staid _____
3 studyed _____
4 tryed _____
5 enjoied _____
6 tidyed _____

VOCABULARY

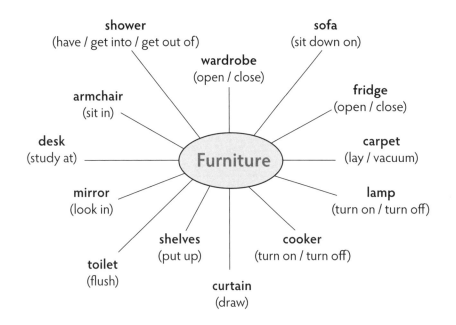

shower
(have / get into / get out of)

sofa
(sit down on)

wardrobe
(open / close)

armchair
(sit in)

fridge
(open / close)

desk
(study at)

Furniture

carpet
(lay / vacuum)

mirror
(look in)

lamp
(turn on / turn off)

shelves
(put up)

cooker
(turn on / turn off)

toilet
(flush)

curtain
(draw)

Look

look up
(a word / a person)

look into
(a crime)

look at
(a picture)

look after
(children / pets)

look for
(your keys)

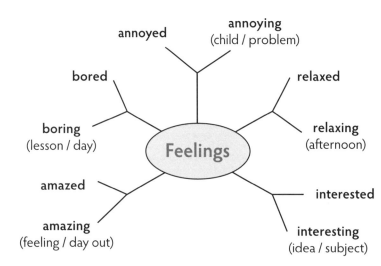

annoying
(child / problem)

annoyed

bored

relaxed

boring
(lesson / day)

Feelings

relaxing
(afternoon)

amazed

interested

amazing
(feeling / day out)

interesting
(idea / subject)

Key words in context

charity	My dad gives money to a **charity** that helps children in poor countries.
creative	She's a writer so she always has very **creative** ideas.
care for	This charity **cares for** dogs that have no home.
work together	Let's **work together** and finish this job quickly.
uncomfortable	This sofa is **uncomfortable**. We need a new one.
comfortable	My bed is really **comfortable**. I don't want to get out of it in the mornings.
untidy	Your room is **untidy**. There are books and clothes all over the floor.
safe	You're **safe** now. There's no danger anymore.
at home	I don't think Bob is **at home**. All the lights are off.
homeless	There are many **homeless** people living on the streets in London.
pay attention	I want you to stop talking and **pay attention** to me.

Furniture SB p.50

1 ★★☆ Use the sentences to complete the crossword.

ACROSS

3 Ian is looking at his hair in the ___.

5 Liam is standing at the ___ in the kitchen making dinner.

8 Tim is putting his clothes in the ___.

10 Don't turn the ___ off. I'm using it to read.

11 Priscilla is washing her hair in the ___.

12 Ollie is doing his homework at his ___.

DOWN

1 The dog is lying on the floor on the ___ in front of the TV.

2 Mum is sitting in the ___ reading the newspaper.

4 Bob is sitting with Sally and Jim on the ___.

6 Ben's little brother over the road is watching us from behind the ___.

7 Dad is putting his books up on the ___.

9 Can I use the ___ before we go out? Yes, it's in the bathroom upstairs.

2 ★★★ What are your favourite pieces of furniture? Choose three pieces and write about each one.

I love the armchair in our living room because it's very comfortable.

1 _____

2 _____

3 _____

-ed and -ing adjectives SB p.53

3 ★☆☆ Find nine more adjectives in the word snake and write them below.

bored)rannoyedcrelaxingfeamazed...

0   *bored*

1 _____

2 _____

3 _____

4 _____

5 _____

6 _____

7 _____

8 _____

9 _____

4 ★★☆ Circle the correct adjective.

0 This sunset is *amazing* / amazed.

1 This lesson is boring / bored.

2 I love holidays. They're so relaxed / relaxing.

3 We broke Mr Evans's window with our ball. I think he is a bit annoying / annoyed with us.

4 I passed the exam! I'm amazing / amazed.

5 Don't turn the TV off, Dad. This programme is really interesting / interested.

WordWise SB p.55
Phrasal verbs with *look*

5 ★☆☆ Match the questions with the replies.

0 What are you looking at? [d]

1 What does 'circulation' mean? [ ]

2 Did you find out what happened to your sandwich? [ ]

3 Do you want to come to my house after school? [ ]

4 What are you looking for? [ ]

a I don't know. Let's look it up in the dictionary.

b I can't. I've got to look after my little brother.

c My pen. I can't find it anywhere.

d Some old photos.

e No – it's a mystery but I'm still looking into it.

6 ★★☆ Circle the correct option to complete the sentences.

0 The police are looking *into* / after / up / for what happened last night.

1 I looked after / up / for / at her number in the phone book.

2 Look up / for / at / into that bird. It's amazing.

3 My mum and dad are looking for / to / into / after a new house.

4 She helps her dad look at / into / after / up her little brothers.

READING

1 REMEMBER AND CHECK Read the article on page 49 of the Student's Book again. What do the numbers refer to?

0 Half past four ___*time*___

1 1,200 _____

2 More than 3 million _____

3 Seven weeks _____

4 17 _____

5 22 _____

2 Read the article quickly, then write the name of the country under the photos.

1 _____

2 _____

3 _____

Some of us live in big houses, some of us live in small houses. Some of us live in apartments in very tall buildings, some of us live in bungalows next to the sea. But most of us live in houses that look like … well … houses. But not everyone. Some people like things that are a bit different and that includes their home. For example, there's a house that looks like a strawberry in Japan, another one that looks like a mushroom in Ohio, USA, and there's a toilet-shaped house in South Korea. There's even a house in Poland that is completely upside down!

Maybe you know the children's poem about the old lady who lived in a shoe. In Pennsylvania, USA there is a real shoe house. Of course, it's not really a shoe, just a house in the shape of a shoe. A local shoe manufacturer called Mahlon N. Haines had the idea of building it. He used it as a guesthouse. When he died it became an ice cream shop for a while. These days, it's a museum.

The One Log House in Garberville, California, USA is a one-bedroom house inside the trunk of a 2,000-year-old giant redwood tree. It took two people seven months to remove all the inside of the tree and make a living space that is just over two metres high and nearly 10 metres long.

Joanne Ussary from Benoit, Mississippi in the USA lives in a plane. It's a Boeing 727, without the wings. The plane cost $2,000 and it cost another $4,000 to move it on to her land. She spent another $24,000 making it into a home.

It's not the only 'flying' home in the USA. In Chattanooga there is a house in the shape of a spaceship; a round white disc with four legs.

And believe it or not, there is a walking house in Denmark. It's a hexagonal tube supported by six metal legs. It can move over most surfaces. It is a collaboration between Danish artists and scientists. Moving home couldn't be any easier. When you want to live somewhere new, just push a button and walk your house to a new location.

3 Read the article again. Answer the questions.

0 What is the shoe house in Pennsylvania today? ___*It's a museum.*___

1 How old is the tree trunk of the One Log House? _____

2 How much did Joanne Ussary spend on turning the plane into a home? _____

3 Who built the walking house in Denmark? _____

4 Which two houses have legs and how many legs have they got? _____

5 How many houses in the article are in the USA? _____

DEVELOPING WRITING

A blog

1 Read the blog entry. Tick (✓) the things that Mia writes about.

POSTED: TUESDAY 5 JANUARY

Welcome to my world – my room

Next to the bathroom at the top of the stairs in my house is a very special room. It's a small but cosy room. It's a special room because it's the place where I feel most at home in the whole world. It's my bedroom.

I love my bedroom. It's bright and friendly. The walls are light blue and it's got a big window. The sun shines through it every morning. There's a comfortable blue bed, a small wooden desk and some shelves where I keep all my favourite books. On the walls there are some really cool posters of my favourite films.

I always feel really relaxed in my bedroom. It's the only room in the house where I can be on my own, away from all the noise of my family. I always go there to do my homework, read a book, listen to music or just to lie on the bed and think. I never feel bored in my bedroom.

Labels: my room, special place   **16 comments**

2 Complete the sentences from the text with the missing adjectives.

0   It's a ___*small*___ but ___*cosy*___ room.

1   I love my bedroom. It's _____ and

     _____ .

2   There's a _____ _____ bed

3   A _____ _____ desk.

Writing tip: adjectives

- We can use more than one adjective to make our writing more descriptive.
- If the adjectives come after the noun or pronoun we use *and* or *but* to separate them. Look at example sentences 0 and 1. Why do we use *but* in sentence 0 and *and* in sentence 1?
- If the adjectives come before the noun we don't use *and*, however, we need to be careful about the order we use them. The usual order is: my opinion / size / colour / what it's made of.
- Try not to use more than two adjectives.

3 Look at the three paragraphs of Mia's blog. Which paragraph …

a   describes the room?

b   talks about how the room makes Mia feel?

c   introduces the room and says where it is?

4 Think about your favourite room.

1   Where is it?

     _____

2   Describe it. What's it got inside?

     _____

3   How do you feel when you are there? Why?

     _____

4   Think of some good adjectives to use.

     _____

5 Write a blog about your favourite room in about 100–130 words. Use Mia's blog and the language above to help you.

LISTENING

1 🔊**23** Listen to Dan and Emily talking about raising money. Tick (✓) the things they talk about.

 1 ☐

 2 ☐

 3 ☐ TOYS

 4 ☐ BOOKS

 5 ☐

 6 ☐

2 🔊**23** Listen again and complete the sentences with no more than four words.

0 They want to raise money for people who lost
   their homes in an earthquake in China.

1 Danny wants to raise _____ of money.

2 Most of Emily's toys _____ or have bits missing.

3 Danny thinks that most people use
   _____ to clean their cars.

4 Tickets for the rock festival will cost
   _____ .

5 They can use the _____ for the rock festival.

6 They need to get permission _____ for the festival.

DIALOGUE

1 Put the words and phrases in order to make parts of the dialogue.

0 **DANNY** to raise / something / money / let's do / a lot of

   Let's do something to raise a lot of money.

1 **EMILY** we could / think / do you ?

   _____

2 **DANNY** and sell / we get / old toys / why don't / all our / them?

   _____

3 **EMILY** not / so / I'm / sure.

   _____

4 **EMILY** their cars / going round / how about / and washing / for them / to people's houses ?

   _____

5 **DANNY** think / good idea / that's a / I don't

   _____

PHRASES FOR FLUENCY `SB p.55`

1 Put the dialogue in order.

☐ **A** Oh no! But I know what you mean – he gets angry really easily.

1 **A** Did Chris invite you to his party?

☐ **A** Well, I hope you come anyway.

☐ **A** What did you say?

☐ **A** Hang on. Why not? I thought you were friends.

☐ **B** We were. But I said something he didn't like and now he doesn't talk to me.

☐ **B** No he didn't. It's no big deal, though.

☐ **B** To be honest, I don't want to.

☐ **B** I just said he wasn't a very good footballer. He got really angry with me.

☐ **B** Anyway, it's not my problem he's angry. And I really don't care about his silly party.

2 Complete the sentences. Use words in the list.

~~deal~~ | honest | problem | hang | mean | though

1 **A** Why are you so annoyed? It's really not a big
   deal .

   B Maybe It Isn't. I'm still angry, _____ .

2 **A** I don't want to go to the match, to be
   _____ . I don't really like football.

   B I know what you _____ . It is really boring.

3 **A** _____ on. We can't just leave this dog here on the street.

   B Of course we can. It's not our _____ .

Reading and Writing part 5

1 Read the article about home. Choose the best word (A, B or C) for each space.

What is a home?

For ⁰_____ home is a place where I feel safe at all times. It is a place where I always feel welcome. It is always full of friends ¹_____ family. Home is more than just a house. It's the street where I live too. It's the park ²_____ the bottom of the road. It's the shops where I ³_____ my comic every week and where I get my crisps and sweets. When I walk down ⁴_____ streets, I see the friendly faces of people who know my name and say 'hello'. I stop to talk to these people to find out what is ⁵_____ in their lives. They ⁶_____ me questions about my life too.

When someone stops and asks me for directions I know where he ⁷_____ to go and I can tell him the best way to get there. Home is a place where I ⁸_____ ask other people for directions.

Example:

0	A mine	B my	**C** me		
1	A and	B so	C but		
2	A in	B at	C over		
3	A bought	B buy	C buys		
4	A that	B this	C these		
5	A happen	B happened	C happening		
6	A ask	B say	C tell		
7	A want	B wanted	C wants		
8	A always	B sometimes	C never		

Exam guide: multiple-choice cloze

In a multiple-choice cloze, you are given three choices of words that could fit the gap to complete a text. You must select the correct one.

- Read all the text to understand what it is about.
- Look at each gap carefully. Look at the words before and after it. Can you guess what word is missing without looking at the answers? If your guess is one of the options, then it is probably the correct answer.
- If you can't guess the word, look at the answers. Put each one in the gap and read the sentence to yourself in your head. Which one sounds correct?
- If you are not sure which is the correct word, then cross out the ones that don't sound right and choose one of the others.
- Always choose an answer even if you have no idea which one is correct.

2 Read the story. Choose the best word (A, B or C) for each space.

Last week my mum and dad decided to get a cleaner to come and clean the house ⁰_____ a week. They both work and they don't have ¹_____ time to do the housework. They arranged for the cleaner to come ²_____ Monday morning. I was very surprised when my dad asked ³_____ to tidy my room on the Sunday. 'What about the cleaner?' I asked. 'We have to tidy a bit,' he said. 'The house ⁴_____ a mess.' So I tidied my room, Mum tidied the rest of the house and Dad vacuumed. Then Dad started cleaning the windows and Mum started cleaning the fridge and the cooker and the rest of the ⁵_____ . They cleaned from morning to evening and when they finished the house ⁶_____ sparkling clean. The next morning the cleaner came. I went ⁷_____ school and Mum and Dad went to work. When we got home later in the afternoon there ⁸_____ a note on the kitchen table. It was from the cleaner. 'I'm sorry,' it read, 'I can't clean your house. There is nothing to clean!'

Example:

0	A one	B first	**C** once
1	A much	B many	C lots
2	A in	B at	C on
3	A I	B me	C my
4	A is	B was	C be
5	A bedroom	B bathroom	C kitchen
6	A were	B is	C was
7	A for	B in	C to
8	A is	B was	C were

6 BEST FRIENDS

GRAMMAR

Past simple (irregular verbs) SB p.58

1 ★ ☆ ☆ Write the past simple forms of these verbs. Use the irregular verb list on page 128.

0	know	*knew*	6	drink _____
1	buy	_____	7	have _____
2	bring	_____	8	say _____
3	take	_____	9	tell _____
4	eat	_____	10	get _____
5	leave	_____	11	cost _____

2 ★★ ☆ Complete the crossword.

ACROSS

1 Yesterday we _____ a really good film.

4 His name is Bill? Really? I _____ it was Brian.

8 We met last year. We _____ really good friends.

9 It was my sister's birthday. I _____ her a CD.

10 Last night I _____ my homework.

DOWN

1 My dad played the guitar and I _____ a song.

2 I _____ to the cinema three times last week.

3 I liked the blue shirt and the red one. In the end I _____ the red one.

5 We had a party last night. We _____ a lot of noise!

6 We _____ a strange noise, but it was only the wind.

7 When he came in to the room, everyone _____ up.

8 The match _____ at three o'clock.

3 ★★★ Complete the text with the verbs in brackets in the past simple form. (Careful! Some verbs are regular and some are irregular).

It was hard to believe, but it was true – a concert by Kings of Leon, in our town! When I ⁰ *saw* (see) the poster, I ¹_____ (phone) all my friends to tell them. At first they ²_____ (not believe) me, but then they all ³_____ (get) really excited!

We all really ⁴_____ (want) to go to the concert – it was our favourite band and we ⁵_____ (hear) that you could buy tickets online. The tickets were too expensive, I ⁶_____ (not have) enough money, but my dad ⁷_____ (give) me some money as an early birthday present and we ⁸_____ (buy) four tickets near the stage.

We were all very excited. For two weeks we ⁹_____ (not talk) about anything else – just the concert. And then finally, the big day ¹⁰_____ (arrive). My friends ¹¹_____ (come) to my house and we all ¹²_____ (get) ready. Then we ¹³_____ (take) a bus to go to the concert.

We ¹⁴_____ (have) a great time at the concert. The band ¹⁵_____ (play) really well and they ¹⁶_____ (perform) for three hours! My friends and I ¹⁷_____ (sing) too, because we ¹⁸_____ (know) the words to every song! Unfortunately they ¹⁹_____ (not sing) my favourite song, but you can't have everything, I guess.

After the show we all ²⁰_____ (go) to a fast food place. We ²¹_____ (eat) hamburgers and ²²_____ (talk) about the show. Allie ²³_____ (say) it was the best concert ever – and we ²⁴_____ (think) the same!

Double genitive SB p.59

4 ★★ **For each sentence, circle the correct answer (A, B or C).**

0   Last week I met a friend of ... .
A you   B your   **C yours**

1   He gave me a jacket of ... .
A him   B his   C he

2   Oh, yes, Jack and Sue are very good friends of ... .
A ours   B our   C us

3   I don't know her, but she's a cousin of ... .
A Johns'   B John's   C John

4   I love their music. I've got eight CDs of ... .
A them   B their   C theirs

5   I found out that our teacher is an old friend of ... .
A my father's B me father   C my father

Past simple: questions   SB p.61

5 ★★ **Use the words in brackets to form questions. Then use the information in brackets to write the answers.**

0   _Did you like_ the film yesterday? (you / like)
    Yes, I did. (✓)

1   _____ any clothes at the weekend?
(he / buy)
    _____ (✗)

2   _____ a lot of photos last weekend?
(you / take)
    _____ (✗)

3   _____ with you to the party? (your friends / go)
    _____ (✓)

4   Who _____ in town this morning? (you / see)
    _____ (Jenny)

5   Where _____ on holiday last year?
(they / go)
    _____ (Corfu)

6   What _____ for dinner last night? (you / eat)
    _____ (pizza)

6 ★★★ **Complete the questions.**

0   I saw someone yesterday.
Who _did you see_ ?

1   I bought something last week.
What _____ ?

2   They went somewhere last weekend.
Where _____ ?

3   I heard something.
What _____ ?

4   You said something.
What _____ ?

5   She told me something.
What _____ ?

6   I met someone.
Who _____ ?

7   I found the answer somewhere.
Where _____ ?

8   I phoned her last night.
Who _____ ?

GET IT RIGHT! 👁
Past simple: questions

We form past simple questions with question word + *did* + subject + base form of the verb. Remember to use *did* in the correct place.

✓ Where **did you meet** your friend?
✗ Where ~~you met~~ your friend?
✗ Where ~~you did meet~~ your friend?

Write a cross (✗) next to the incorrect sentences. Then write the correct sentences.

1   Why you didn't come to my party?   ☐
    _____

2   What you did at the weekend?   ☐
    _____

3   Where did they go on holiday?   ☐
    _____

4   Who you went to the cinema with?   ☐
    _____

5   What he saw at the cinema?   ☐
    _____

VOCABULARY

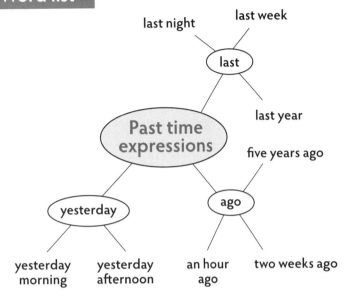

last night
last week
last
last year
five years ago
Past time expressions
yesterday
ago
yesterday morning
yesterday afternoon
an hour ago
two weeks ago

Irregular past participles

buy	bought
come	came
choose	chose
find	found
give	gave
get	got
have	had
leave	left
make	made
say	said
see	saw
stand	stood
think	thought
take	took
go	went

cheerful
confident
boring
easy-going
jealous
Personality adjectives
funny
intelligent
generous
horrible
helpful

Possessive pronouns

I	mine
you	yours
he	his
she	hers
it	its
we	ours
they	theirs

Key words in context

certainly	I love parties, so I will **certainly** come to yours!
friendship	It was the start of a great **friendship**.
go surfing	It's a great day to **go surfing** – look at the sea!
have an accident	Be careful when you cross the street – I don't want you to **have an accident**.
in public	It's OK to do that at home, but not **in public**!
myth	A lot of people think it's true, but it isn't – it's just a **myth**.
patient	I know you're hungry, but be **patient** – dinner will be ready in 15 minutes.
right now	No, I can't wait – I want it **right now**!
save someone's life	Firemen often **save people's lives**.
score	The final **score** was 3–1.
stressed	It's an important exam, so I'm a bit **stressed** right now.
upset	It was very bad news, so she was **upset**.

Past time expressions SB p.58

1 ★ ☆ ☆ (Circle) the correct option.

0 I saw her two weeks (ago)/ yesterday.
1 Where were you *last / yesterday* afternoon?
2 He arrived *last / yesterday* week.
3 We started school five years *ago / last*.
4 I tried to phone you three hours *ago / afternoon*.
5 I didn't feel well *last / yesterday* morning.
6 We went out *last / yesterday* night.

2 ★★ ☆ Complete the puzzle. What is the 'mystery word'?

	0	L	A	S	T		

0 We went to the cinema ___last___ Sunday.
1 The time now is 7.25. _____ minutes ago, it was 7.10.
2 Today is Monday. _____ was Sunday.
3 It's 25th August. Two _____ ago it was the 11th.
4 I was late for school this _____ .
5 I watched a great film last _____ .
6 I was born fifteen years _____ .
7 It's December. _____ months ago it was October.
8 We went out to a restaurant yesterday _____ .

3 ★★★ Complete each sentence about you / your family / your country, or anything / anyone else you know.

0 Two years ago, *my sister got married* .
1 Last night, _____ .
2 Three weeks ago, _____ .
3 _____ an hour ago.
4 Fifty years ago, _____ .
5 Last Sunday, _____ .
6 _____ yesterday morning.
7 Last year, _____ .
8 Yesterday afternoon _____ .

Character adjectives SB p.61

4 ★★ ☆ Complete the adjectives and then match them with the definitions a–i.

0 f u n n y — f
1 _ _ _ p f _ _ — ☐
2 _ t _ _ l _ _ _ t — ☐
3 _ h _ _ _ f _ _ — ☐
4 _ _ _ _ y-_ _ _ n _ — ☐
5 g _ _ _ _ _ _ u _ — ☐
6 _ _ _ f _ d _ _ _ — ☐
7 _ _ a l _ _ s — ☐
8 b _ _ i _ _ — ☐

a relaxed and not easily worried
b happy and positive
c unhappy because you want something someone else has
d happy to give other people money, presents or time
e not interesting or exciting
f making you smile or laugh
g certain about your ability to do things well
h happy to help others
i able to learn and understand things easily

5 ★★ ☆ Look at these character adjectives. Which ones do you think are positive (P), or negative (N)?

☐ cheerful   ☐ confident
☐ easy-going   ☐ funny
☐ horrible   ☐ generous
☐ helpful   ☐ jealous
☐ intelligent   ☐ boring

6 ★★ ☆ Choose four adjectives from Exercise 5. Write sentences about yourself.

I'm usually a cheerful person.
I'm not really jealous at all.

Pronunciation
Stressed syllables in words
Go to page 119.

READING

1 REMEMBER AND CHECK For each sentence, circle the correct option. Then check your answers in the article on page 57 of the Student's Book.

0 *Charlotte* / *The music teacher* suggested that the two friends could sing together.

1 Jonathan wasn't sure about going on TV because of his *appearance* / *voice*.

2 When they came onto the stage they were very *relaxed* / *nervous*.

3 One judge on the TV show said that *Jonathan* / *Charlotte* should sing alone.

4 They *won* / *came second in* the TV competition.

5 Their first CD was called *Two of Us* / *Together*.

2 How many of the friends in the photos can you name? Read the text quickly and check your ideas.

Famous friends in literature

As we all know, having friends is really important in our lives. But of course there are also great friendships in books and films – and some of them are very famous.

In JK Rowling's books, Harry Potter's two great friends are Hermione and Ron. Harry relies on them a lot and they often help him in difficult situations. And though they don't always all agree on everything, they're friends for life.

Back in the nineteenth century, an American writer called Mark Twain created two characters called Tom Sawyer and Huckleberry Finn. They lived in southern USA near the Mississippi River. Together they had problems with their families and with slavery.

Also in the nineteenth century, in Britain, Sir Arthur Conan Doyle created one of the most famous detectives ever: Sherlock Holmes. His friend, Dr Watson became very famous too … and Watson always tried to help Holmes. In a recent film, the two friends were played by Robert Downey Junior and Jude Law.

Meanwhile in 1844, over in France, Alexandre Dumas wrote *The Three Musketeers*. The characters Athos, Aramis and Porthos were in a special part of the King's Army and fought against injustice. Together with D'Artagnan, they showed their friendship with a cry of: 'All for one, and one for all!' These famous friends have also appeared in films on many occasions over the years.

OK, so what about a friendship between a boy and a bear? That's what we saw in the film of Rudyard Kipling's famous story *The Jungle Book*. Mowgli is a small orphan boy. He was found in the jungle and looked after by wolves. His great friend is an easy-going bear, Baloo. He helps Mowgli in his fight against the dangerous tiger, Shere Khan.

There are many stories about friendships between men or boys (and there's Baloo too), but famous stories about friends don't seem to include many girls or women. There's *Little Women*, of course – Louisa May Alcott's story of four sisters in New England and how they love each other, but they were sisters and not just friends. Has anyone out there got some great female literary friendships, please?

3 Read the text again. Answer the questions.

1 Who are Harry Potter's friends?

_____

2 When did Mark Twain write his stories about two friends?

_____

3 Which friends shouted: 'All for one, and one for all'?

_____

4 What did Baloo help Mowgli to do?

_____

5 Why is *Little Women* different from other examples of friends?

_____

4 Do you know any other famous friendships in stories or in films, or on TV? Write two sentences.

I read a book where there are three friends called ...

_____

_____

I saw a film ...

_____

_____

DEVELOPING WRITING

An apology

1 Read the messages. Match them with the answers. There is one extra answer!

Hello Thomas,

I'm sorry I didn't come to your birthday party. My aunt and uncle came to visit us on Saturday, and Kylie and James, my cousins, were with them. We always get on very well with each other. To be honest we were all together and when I remembered about your party it was too late. I didn't want to phone you, so I'm writing to explain what happened. I hope you can forgive me! I'm really sorry.

Jeremy

B

Hi Clare,

I'm writing to say I'm so sorry about what happened last week. I don't know why we started to fight. I'm really sorry for the things I said. I hope we can still be friends because I really like you. Oh, I've got tickets for the concert on Sunday. Would you like to come with me? Please say yes.

John

C

Dear Joanne,

Sorry about what I said yesterday about people who use mobile phones all the time. I really didn't know that your grandma was ill. I understand you wanted to phone her, and I'm really sorry that I hurt you. I hope you're not angry with me any more. I made a mistake, but I really didn't want to hurt you.

Love,
Karen

A

☐ **1** Hi … , Thanks for telling me. I didn't understand why you didn't come to the party. Now I do and I'm not angry because we all make mistakes. Next time – don't forget!

☐ **2** Hi … , How could I be angry? Your message is so funny! It's OK you forgot about the money. Let's not talk about it any more. I can't wait to see your present.

☐ **3** Hi … , Thanks for writing. Do you know what? I kind of feel the same. There wasn't really a reason to start a fight. And, yes, we are normally great friends. Thanks for the invitation, but I can't come. It's my dad's birthday this weekend.

☐ **4** Hi … , Thanks so much for writing. I'm really not happy myself when people have their mobiles on all the time. Only it was different for me this time. Thanks for understanding! I hope we can meet soon.

Writing tip: informal messages

When you send an email or another message to a friend, use an informal style of writing.

- Begin your message with *Hi* (name), or *Hello* (name). You can use *Dear* (name) in informal and formal messages.
- Use short forms, e.g. *I'm, We didn't, you aren't*, etc.
- Make it personal. For example, use sentences such as: *I'm sorry about what happened. I hope we can still be friends. You know I really like you. Please say yes.*
- End your message with one of the following: *Love,* (name); *Cheers,* (name); *Take care,* (name); *Hope to hear from you soon,* (name); or use only your name.

2 Write an email to apologise. Choose one of the following situations.

I'm so sorry!

LISTENING

1 🔊26 Samantha is telling Jack about a man and his cat. Listen and find out their names.

2 🔊26 Listen again. (Circle) the correct answers.

1 At first, Jack …
  A thinks the story of the cat is very interesting.
  B thinks Samantha's telling him a joke.
  C isn't interested in the story.

2 James became a writer. His book is about …
  A the time when he played music for little money.
  B how his friendship with a cat changed his life.
  C people in London and their pets.

3 Bob the Cat …
  A is now well known and may become a film star.
  B can do some tricks and play the guitar.
  C is now living in a home for street animals.

4 Jack would like to …
  A have a cat like Bob.
  B watch the film about Bob.
  C read the book too.

3 🔊26 Listen again. Complete each space with between one and three words.

1 James was a street musician, sitting on _____ and playing his guitar.

2 When James saw the cat for the first time, it had a problem with _____ .

3 When James went home on the underground, the cat _____ him.

4 When James had the cat near him, more people stopped and gave him _____ money.

5 James decided to write a book about his _____ the cat.

6 Samantha thinks that about _____ people bought
A Street Cat named Bob.

DIALOGUE

1 🔊27 Listen to the sentences. Write the past tense verb you hear in the spaces. Then put the sentences in the correct order.

[1] A What _____*did*_____ you do in London at the weekend?

☐ B Indian food? I'm sure you _____ Indian. I know it's your favourite.

☐ C And what _____ that?

☐ D Yes, it's delicious, isn't it? And I'm sure you _____ lots of things as well.

☐ E Well, yes, I _____ some nice clothes in the shops but I only _____ one thing.

☐ F Oh, we _____ lots of things. And we _____ some great food.

☐ G Of course! But we _____ some Chinese food, too. That _____ nice.

☐ H I _____ this belt. It's for you. I'm sorry I _____ your birthday last week!

■ TRAIN TO THiNK ■

Making decisions

1 You can invite a famous person to your birthday party. Who do you want? Write the names of three people you like in the circles.

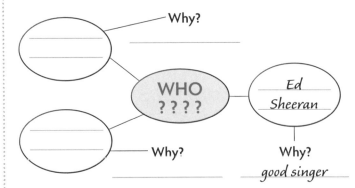

2 Next to each person write one reason for inviting him/her.

3 Use your mind map to make a decision.

4 Write a sentence saying who you want and why.
  I want Ed Sheeran because he can sing for me.

CAMBRIDGE ENGLISH: Key

Listening part 2

1 🔊28 Listen to Kevin telling Abigail about his birthday. What present did each person give him? For questions 1–5, write a letter A–H next to each person.

People		Presents	
0 Brother	C	A	book
1 Sister	☐	B	sports shoes
2 Mum	☐	C	DVD
3 Dad	☐	D	tickets
4 Aunt	☐	E	camera
5 Granddad	☐	F	video game
		G	laptop
		H	money

Exam guide: matching

In Listening part 2 you are given a list of five items, and a list of eight different items. You must listen to a dialogue and match each of the five items with an item from the other list.

- Before listening, quickly read through the two lists.
- Listen carefully – the first object you hear is not always the correct answer. In the example above, you hear:

    Abigail: What did you get from your sister?

    Kevin: Well, she usually gives me a book, but this time she bought me this video game. It's a sports game. It's great fun to play.

- Sometimes, you will not hear exactly the object you see in the list, but a 'paraphrase' – a word or group of words that mean the same as another word. In the example below from Exercise 1 when Kevin says *trainers* he is talking about *sports shoes*. Example:

    Abigail: Oh! And what did your mum give you? Some money?

    Kevin: No, she bought me these <u>trainers</u>? Do you like them?

2 🔊29 Listen to Charlotte talking to her friend Christian about a photo of her old school friends. What clothes were her friends wearing? For questions 1–5, write a letter A–H next to each person.

People		Their clothes	
0 Ella	G	A	jacket
1 Jacob	☐	B	trousers
2 Olivia	☐	C	belt
3 Cynthia	☐	D	jumper
4 Sylvia	☐	E	shorts
5 Adam	☐	F	trainers
		G	dress
		H	shirt

Reading and Writing part 2

1 Read the sentences about a TV talent show. Choose the best word (A, B or C) for each space.

1 Last year I _____ to enter a talent show.
   A decided   B realised   C thought

2 I sang a song in front of three _____ .
   A audience   B contestants   C judges

Exam guide: multiple-choice sentences

In Reading and Writing part 2 you have to complete a sentence from a choice of three words. The sentences are all about the same topic or tell a simple story. This exercise tests vocabulary, not grammar.

- Read the sentence without looking at the words. Try to guess what the missing word is.
- Check the words. Is the word you guessed one of them? If it is, then that is probably the correct answer.
- If the word you guessed isn't one of the options, read the sentence in your head and put each of the words in turn into the gap. Which word sounds best?

2 Read the sentences about friends. Choose the best word (A, B or C) for each space.

0 Steve and Allan are _____ friends.
   Ⓐ best   B first   C better

1 They _____ at school when they were five years old.
   A made   B met   C knew

2 They get _____ really well.
   A on   B over   C together

3 They're really _____ friends and they share all their secrets.
   A near   B far   C close

4 They never fight or _____ arguments.
   A do   B make   C have

5 They have a great _____ .
   A friends   B friendly   C friendship

61

CONSOLIDATION

LISTENING

1 🔊30 **Listen and tick (✓) the correct room.**

A ☐

B ☐

C ☐

2 🔊30 **Listen again and answer the questions.**

1   Why does she like blue walls?
2   Why does she like the fact that her desk is near the window?
3   When did she get her new wardrobe?
4   Who gave her the money for the wardrobe?
5   How did they know that she didn't like her old wardrobe?
6   How does her sister feel about the new wardrobe?

GRAMMAR

3 **Complete the conversation. Put the verbs in brackets into the correct form of the past simple.**

JASON   I ⁰___went___ (go) to a party at Jack's house on Friday. It was great.

PAUL   Good. I'm happy that you ¹_____ (like) it. Jack's parties are good fun.

JASON   Yes, they are. I ²_____ (dance) with Alison Gardner. We ³_____ (have) a great time there!

PAUL   Yes, Alison's nice. I ⁴_____ (take) her to the cinema three weeks ago. We ⁵_____ (see) a great film.

JASON   That's nice. But you ⁶_____ (not go) to Jack's party! Why not?

PAUL   Jack ⁷_____ (not invite) me. He ⁸_____ (have) another party two months ago, and he ⁹_____ (invite) me to that.

JASON   Two months ago? I ¹⁰_____ (not know) that! Now I'm annoyed!

PAUL   Oh. I ¹¹_____ (say) the wrong thing. Sorry.

VOCABULARY

4 **Complete each adjective. The first letter is already there.**

0   She always understands what's happening.
She's very i _n t e l l i g e n t_ .

1   I'm sure I passed the exam. I'm very c _ _ _ _ _ _ _ _ _ about it.

2   The film was awful! I was really b _ _ _ _ _ .

3   I love the new mirror in your room! I'm really j _ _ _ _ _ _ _ !

4   After a long day, I like to have a long, r _ _ _ _ _ _ _ _ shower!

5   I was late with my homework again. The teacher was quite a _ _ _ _ _ _ _ with me.

6   He looks sad today. He usually smiles and looks c _ _ _ _ _ _ _ _ _ .

7   The game yesterday was great – really a _ _ _ _ _ _ _ ! I loved it.

8   She was very h _ _ _ _ _ _ _ and painted my room with me.

5 (Circle) **the correct options.**

Near our town there's a famous old house where some rich people lived about two hundred years ⁰*last* / (*ago*). Last weekend my mum said, '¹*Why* / *How* about going to visit that house?' And we did. I brought a friend of ²*my* / *mine* with us. We ³*went* / *go* by bus and my mum ⁴*paid* / *took* for us all to go in. I didn't really want to go at first because I'm usually ⁵*boring* / *bored* by museums and things. But when we got there, I thought it was ⁶*amazing* / *amazed*.

The house has got about sixty rooms and they were really ⁷*interesting* / *intelligent*. There was an enormous ⁸*sofa* / *desk* – I'm sure twenty people could sit on it! The windows were really big with beautiful red ⁹*carpets* / *curtains* on them. My dad ¹⁰*took* / *take* a photograph in one of the rooms, but a man working there got ¹¹*annoyed* / *annoying* because there was a sign that said: 'No photographs!'

DIALOGUE

6 **Complete the conversation. Use the words in the list.**

~~bored~~ | about | ago | boring | could | didn't | enjoy | let's | sure | thought | went | why

MIKE   I'm so ⁰ _bored_

JANINE   How ¹_____ going for a walk?

MIKE   No, I ²_____ for a walk yesterday. ³_____ do something here in the house.

JANINE   A computer game! ⁴_____ don't we play a computer game?

MIKE   No. Do you remember? We played on the computer last Saturday and I ⁵_____ win a single game!

JANINE   Oh yes, I remember! I ⁶_____ it was great fun.

MIKE   Yes. But I didn't ⁷_____ it very much.

JANINE   Sorry, Mike. It's just a joke, OK? But here's an idea. We ⁸_____ watch my new DVD. I bought it two days ⁹_____ .

MIKE   I'm not so ¹⁰_____ . Is it one of those romantic films? They're so ¹¹_____ .

JANINE   No, don't worry. It's an adventure. Come on, let's try it.

READING

7 **Read this newspaper article about making decisions. Circle the correct ending (A or B) for each sentence.**

1 Psychologists at a university in the USA wanted to find out

   A if teenagers and their friends are good car drivers.

   B what decisions teenagers make when they are with friends.

2 They noticed that teenagers behaved in a more dangerous way when

   A they thought their friends were not watching.

   B they thought their friends were watching them.

3 The experiments show that teenagers need to be careful about making decisions when

   A they are with their friends.

   B they are on their own.

WRITING

8 **Write a paragraph about you and your decisions in about 80 words. Use the questions to help you.**

● How often do you make decisions? What type of decisions are easy / difficult?

● Do you ever ask for advice when making a decision?

● With your friends do you make decisions for the group or does someone else?

_____

_____

_____

_____

_____

_____

When teens make BAD DECISIONS

PSYCHOLOGISTS at Temple University in Philadelphia, USA did an interesting experiment. They asked teenagers to play a video game that involved car driving. They could win prizes for driving fast. But the faster they drove, the bigger their risk was of losing the prize money. Half the time, the teenagers played the game on their own, and half of the time the psychologists told them that their friends were in the room next door, watching them. The results were fascinating: when the teens played the game on their own, they made much better decisions. When they thought their friends were watching, their driving was much more dangerous. They drove faster, had more accidents, and often didn't stop at red lights.

Psychologists say that teens should think carefully before making important decisions when their friends are present!

PRONUNCIATION

UNIT 1
Plurals and third person verb endings: /s/, /z/ or /ɪz/

1   Add -*s* or -*es* to the present simple verbs. Write them in the correct column.

~~cook~~ | dance | enjoy | finish
give | need | play | relax | sleep | swim
take | want | wash | watch | write

/s/ – works	/z/ – lives	/ɪz/ – closes
cooks		

2   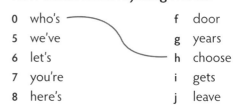 04   Listen, check and repeat.

3   Complete the sentences with the plural nouns.

~~blogs~~ | bikes | buses | cats | players
puzzles | stamps | quizzes

0   Jane enjoys writing cooking and sport _*blogs*_ . /z/

1   Julie's favourite games are crosswords and _____ . /z/

2   Luke's got lots of pets – a dog, some fish and four black and white _____ . /s/

3   The girls in that team are all good _____ . /z/

4   Julie watches _____ on TV. /ɪz/

5   Many students like riding their _____ in the park. /s/

6   Jenny catches the red _____ in London. /ɪz/

7   Lewis collects _____ and bottle tops. /s/

4   04 05   Listen, check and repeat.

UNIT 2
Contractions

1   Match the rhyming words.

0   I'm   a   here
1   she's   b   time
2   they're   c   chair
3   it's   d   please
4   we're   e   sits

2   07   Listen, check and repeat.

3   Now match these rhyming words.

0   who's   f   door
5   we've   g   years
6   let's   h   choose
7   you're   i   gets
8   here's   j   leave

4   08   Listen, check and repeat.

UNIT 3
Vowel sounds: /ɪ/ and /iː/

1   14   Put your finger on *Start*. Listen to the words. Go left if you hear the /ɪ/ sound and right if you hear the /iː/ sound. Say the name. You'll hear the words twice.

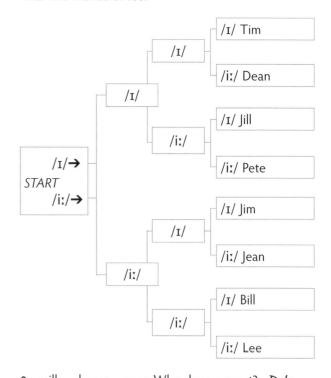

0   milk – cheese – peas. Who do you meet? _*Pete*_

1 _____   2 _____   3 _____   4 _____   5 _____

2   15   Listen, check and repeat.

UNIT 4
er /ə/ at the end of words

1 Complete the sentences with the words in the list.

~~later~~ | after | answer | daughter
father | other | paper | writer

0 Ten minutes ___*later*___ an ambulance was there.

1 My friend Sara wants to be a _____.

2 I don't know the _____ to that question.

3 Our teacher always asks us to speak to each _____ in English.

4 Please write your answers on a separate piece of _____.

5 That little girl over there is Mr Power's _____.

6 My _____'s a farmer. He works very hard.

7 Can you come to my house _____ school?

2 ◄))16 Listen, check and repeat.

UNIT 5
Regular past tense endings

1 How many syllables are there? Write them in the columns.

~~asked~~ | closed | ~~rested~~ | missed | needed
played | shouted | started | tried | wanted

one syllable /d/ or /t/	two syllables /ɪd/
asked	rested

2 ◄))21 Listen, check and repeat.

3 Circle the correct words to complete the rule.

The -ed endings of regular verbs in the past simple are ¹*pronounced as a separate syllable / not pronounced as a separate syllable*, /ɪd/ when the infinitive form of the verb ends in /t/ or /d/ only.

In all other cases, the -ed endings are ²*pronounced as a separate syllable / not pronounced as a separate syllable*, but as /t/ or /d/.

4 Write the words ending in the /t/ and /d/ sounds in the correct column.

~~carried~~ | ~~cooked~~ | enjoyed | finished | helped
loved | stayed | tried | worked | washed

/t/ – ask**ed**	/d/ – clos**ed**
cooked	carried

5 ◄))22 Listen, check and repeat.

UNIT 6
Stressed syllables in words

1 Write the words in the correct columns.

~~adventurous~~ | confident | friendly | interesting
good | helpful | intelligent | nice

1	One syllable	2	Two syllables

3	Three syllables	4	Four syllables
			adventurous

2 ◄))24 Listen, check and repeat.

3 Which syllable is stressed? Write the words in the correct columns.

~~confident~~ | adventurous | interesting | important
relaxing | disappointed | intelligent | easy-going

1 Ooo	2 oOo	3 oOoo	4 ooOo
confident			

4 ◄))25 Listen, check and repeat.

119

GRAMMAR REFERENCE

UNIT 1
Present simple

1 We use the present simple for actions that happen repeatedly or habitually.

*Paul often **goes** to the cinema.*
*We **have** dinner at 8.00 every evening.*

We also use the present simple for things that are always or normally true.

*The sun **comes up** in the east.*
*We **go** to a big school in London.*

2 With most subjects, the present simple is the same as the base form of the verb. However, with a third person singular subject (*he, she, it*), the verb has an *-s* ending.

*I **play** tennis on Saturdays.*
*She **plays** tennis on Saturdays.*

If a verb ends with *-sh, -ch, -ss* or *-x*, we add *-es*.

he watches, she catches, he misses, she fixes

If a verb ends with consonant + *-y*, we change the *-y* to *-i* and add *-es*.

she studies, he worries

If a verb ends with vowel + *-y*, then it is regular.

play – plays, say – says, buy – buys

3 The negative of the present simple is formed with *don't* (*do not*) or *doesn't* (*does not*) + base form of the verb.

*I **don't like** carrots.   She **doesn't like** carrots.*

4 Present simple questions and short answers are formed with *do* or *does*.

***Do** you **like** cats?   Yes, I **do**. / No, I **don't**.*
***Does** Jo **live** here?   Yes, she **does**. / No, she **doesn't**.*

like + -ing

1 After verbs which express likes and dislikes we often use verb + *-ing*.

*We **love watching** films at home.*
*My sister **enjoys reading** travel books.*

2 If a verb ends in *-e*, we drop the *-e* before adding *-ing*.

live → living   ride → riding

If a short verb ends in consonant + vowel + consonant, we double the final consonant before adding *-ing*.

get → getting, shop → shopping, travel → travelling

UNIT 2
Present continuous

1 We use the present continuous for actions that are happening now or around the time of speaking.

*My friends and I **are playing** an online game at the moment.*
*It**'s raining** now.*

2 The present continuous is formed with the present simple of *be* + verb + *-ing*.

*I**'m listening to** music.   I**'m not listening** to music.*
*You**'re walking** very fast!   You **aren't walking** very fast.*
*Alison **is talking** to Jo.   Alison **isn't talking** to Jo.*

3 The question is formed with the present simple of *be* + subject + verb + *-ing*. Short answers are formed using *Yes/No* + pronoun + the correct form of *be* (positive or negative).

*Is Susanna **eating**?   Yes, she **is**. / No, she **isn't**.*
*Are the boys **having** fun?   Yes, they **are**. / No, they **aren't**.*
*What **are** you **doing**?   Why is she **crying**?*

Verbs of perception

Verbs of perception (*taste / smell / look / sound*) are not used in the present continuous when they are used to give an opinion. They are used in the present simple only.

*This hamburger **doesn't taste** very nice.*
*Mmm! The food **smells** fantastic!*
*These trousers **don't look** very good on me.*
*I don't know who the singer is, but she **sounds** wonderful.*

Present simple vs. present continuous

1 We use different time expressions with the present simple and the present continuous.

Present simple: *every day, on Mondays, at the weekend, usually, sometimes, often, never*

Present continuous: *today, right now, at the moment*

*James **usually walks** to school but **today** he**'s taking** the bus.*

2 Some verbs aren't normally used in the continuous form. They are called *state verbs* or *stative verbs* because they talk about a state, not an action. Here are some common examples:

believe, know, understand, remember, want, need, mean, like, hate
*I **believe** you. He **knows** a lot about music.*
*Morgan **wants** to have dinner now.*

UNIT 3
Countable and uncountable nouns

1 Nouns in English are **countable** or **uncountable**.

Countable nouns have both singular and plural forms, for example:
bicycle → **bicycles**, *school* → **schools**, *egg* → **eggs**, *question* → **questions**, *man* → **men**, *woman* → **women**, *child* → **children**, *person* → **people**

But uncountable nouns do not have a plural form. They are always singular, for example:
food, music, money, rice, bread, information

2 **Countable nouns** can take singular or plural verbs.

*That **car is** Japanese.   Those **cars are** Japanese.*
*That **woman works** with me.   Those **women work** with my mum.*

Uncountable nouns always take singular verbs.

*This **food is** horrible.   The **music is** too loud!*

a / an; some / any

1 With singular countable nouns, we can use *a / an* to talk about a specific thing or person.

*They've got **a car**.   She's eating **an orange**.*

2 With plural countable nouns, we use *some* (positive) or *any* (negative).

*I want to buy **some apples**.   We haven't got **any eggs**.*

3 With uncountable nouns, we don't use *a / an* – we use *some / any*, like plural countable nouns.

*Let's listen to **some music**.*
*I don't want **any food**.*

4 We use *some* to talk about an unspecified number or amount. We normally use *some* in positive sentences.

*He bought **some fruit** in town.*

We often use *some* in requests and offers.

*Can I have **some** orange juice, please?*
*Do you want **some** cheese?*

5 We use *any* to talk about an unspecified number or amount. We normally use *any* in negative sentences, and in questions.

*He didn't buy **any fruit**.*
*Is there **any fruit** in the kitchen?*

(How) much and (how) many; a lot of / lots of

1 We use *many* with plural countable nouns and *much* with uncountable nouns.

Countable	Uncountable
She doesn't eat **many vegetables**.	He doesn't eat **much fruit**.
How **many children** have they got?	How **much time** have we got?

2 We usually use *many* and *much* in negative sentences and questions.

*I don't go to **many concerts**.*
*How **many eggs** do you want?*

In positive sentences, we normally use *a lot of* or *lots of*. *A lot of / Lots of* can be used with plural countable nouns and with uncountable nouns.

*Chris has got **lots of / a lot of** DVDs.*
*You can get **lots of / a lot of** information on the Internet.*

too much / too many / not enough + noun

1 If we want to say that the number or amount of something is more than we like or want, we can use *too many* or *too much*. We use *too many* with plural countable nouns, and *too much* with uncountable nouns.

*There are **too many chairs** in the room.*
*There's **too much salt** in my food.*

2 We use *not enough* with plural countable nouns and with uncountable nouns to say that we think more is / are needed.

*There **aren't enough chairs** in the room.*
*There **isn't enough salt** in my food.*

too + adjective / (not) + adjective + enough

1 We use *too* + adjective to say that it's more than we like or want.

*This soup is **too hot**.   The clothes are **too expensive**.*

2 We use *(not)* + adjective + *enough* to say that something is less than we like or want.

*This bag **isn't big enough** to put everything in.*

UNIT 4
Possessive adjectives

1 Here is the list of possessive adjectives:

Subject pronoun: *I, you, he, she, it, we, they*
Possessive adjectives: *my, your, his, her, its, our, their*

2 We use possessive adjectives to say who something belongs to.

***My** name's Jack.   Is he **your brother**?   Look at **his hair**!   **Her bike** is really expensive.*
*The DVD isn't in **its box**.   They love **their cat**.*

Possessive pronouns

1 Here is the list of possessive pronouns:

Possessive adjective: *my, your, his, her, our, their*
Possessive pronoun: *mine, yours, his, hers, ours, theirs*

2 Possessive pronouns can take the place of possessive adjective + noun.

*Is this **your book / yours**? No, it isn't **my book / mine**.*
*I like her hair, but I don't like **his**.*

Whose

When we want to ask a question about who is the owner of something, we use the word *whose*. There are two possible constructions after *whose*.

Whose book is this? or *Whose is this book?*

Possessive *'s*

To talk about possession we can add *'s* to the end of a name / noun.

Annie's bike is really fantastic.
That's my brother's bedroom.

If the name / noun ends in an *-s*, (for example, plural nouns), we add the apostrophe (') after the final *-s*.

That's our neighbours' dog.
I don't like James' shirt.

Past simple of *be* (*was / were*)

1 We use the past simple to talk about actions and events in the past.

2 The past simple of *be* is *was / wasn't* or *were / weren't*.

   I was at school yesterday.   You were late yesterday.
   My sister wasn't there.
   The DVDs weren't very good.

3 Questions with *was / were* are formed by putting the verb before the subject.

   Were you at school yesterday?   Was Maria with you?

UNIT 5
Past simple: regular verbs (positive and negative)

1 In the past simple, regular verbs have an *-ed* ending. The form is the same for all subjects.

   I walked to the park.   You played well yesterday.
   Carla opened the window.

   If a verb ends in *-e*, we add only *-d*.

   like → liked   hate → hated   use → used

   If a verb ends with consonant + *-y*, we change the *-y* to *-i* and add *-ed*.

   study → studied   try → tried   marry → married

   If a short verb ends in consonant + vowel + consonant, we double the final consonant before adding *-ed*.

   stop → stopped   plan → planned   travel → travelled

   If a short verb ends in consonant + vowel + *-y*, it is regular.

   play → played   stay → stayed

2 The past simple negative is formed with *didn't* (*did not*) + base form of the verb. The form is the same for all subjects:

   I / We / She didn't enjoy the film last night.

3 Past time expressions are often used with the past simple.

   Yesterday, yesterday morning, last night, last week, a month ago, two years ago, on Sunday

Modifiers: *very, really, quite*

We use the words *very, really, quite* to say more about an adjective. The words *very* and *really* make an adjective stronger.

The food was good – The food was very good.
The film was exciting – The film was really exciting.

We often use *quite* to say 'a little bit'.

The room was quite small. (= not very small, but a bit small)
The film was quite long. (= not very long, but a bit long)

UNIT 6
Past simple: irregular verbs

A lot of common verbs are irregular. This means that the past simple form is different – they don't have the usual *-ed* ending.

go → went, see → saw, eat → ate, think → thought

The form of the past simple for these verbs is the same for all persons (I / you / he / she / it / we / they).

See page 128 for a list of irregular verbs.

The negative of irregular verbs is formed in the same way as regular verbs: *didn't* (*did not*) + base form of the verb.

We didn't enjoy the concert.
I didn't know the answer to the question.

Past simple: (regular and irregular verbs) questions and short answers

1 Past simple questions and short answers are formed with *did*. The form is the same for regular and irregular verbs.

   Did you talk to Barbara this morning?
   Did you see that great match last night?

2 Short answers are formed with *Yes / No* + pronoun + *did / didn't*.

   Did you like the film? Yes, I did.
   Did she phone you last night? No, she didn't.

Double genitive

We use the double genitive to talk about one of many things that we have. We form it with noun + *of* + possessive pronoun (see Unit 4 above). We can also use noun + *of* + noun with possessive *'s*.

He's a friend of mine. (I have many friends)
They are neighbours of ours. (we have many neighbours).

IRREGULAR VERBS

Base form	Past simple	Past participle
be	was / were	been
become	became	become
begin	began	begun
break	broke	broken
bring	brought	brought
build	built	built
buy	bought	bought
can	could	-
catch	caught	caught
choose	chose	chosen
come	came	come
cost	cost	cost
cut	cut	cut
do	did	done
draw	drew	drawn
drink	drank	drunk
drive	drove	driven
eat	ate	eaten
fall	fell	fallen
feel	felt	felt
find	found	found
fly	flew	flown
forget	forgot	forgotten
get	got	got
give	gave	given
go	went	gone
grow	grew	grown
have	had	had
hear	heard	heard
hit	hit	hit
keep	kept	kept
know	knew	known
leave	left	left

Base form	Past simple	Past participle
lend	lent	lent
lie	lay	lain
lose	lost	lost
make	made	made
mean	meant	meant
meet	met	met
pay	paid	paid
put	put	put
read /riːd/	read /red/	read /red/
ride	rode	ridden
run	ran	run
say	said	said
see	saw	seen
sell	sold	sold
send	sent	sent
show	showed	shown
sing	sang	sung
sit	sat	sat
sleep	slept	slept
speak	spoke	spoken
spend	spent	spent
stand	stood	stood
swim	swam	swum
take	took	taken
teach	taught	taught
tell	told	told
think	thought	thought
throw	threw	thrown
understand	understood	understood
wake	woke	woken
wear	wore	worn
win	won	won
write	wrote	written

Acknowledgements

The authors and publishers acknowledge the following sources of copyright material and are grateful for the permissions granted. While every effort has been made, it has not always been possible to identify the sources of all the material used, or to trace all copyright holders. If any omissions are brought to our notice, we will be happy to include the appropriate acknowledgements on reprinting.

Corpus

Development of this publication has made use of the Cambridge English Corpus (CEC). The CEC is a computer database of contemporary spoken and written English, which currently stands at over one billion words. It includes British English, American English and other varieties of English. It also includes the Cambridge Learner Corpus, developed in collaboration with Cambridge English Language Assessment. Cambridge University Press has built up the CEC to provide evidence about language use that helps to produce better language teaching materials.

English Profile

This product is informed by the English Vocabulary Profile, built as part of English Profile, a collaborative programme designed to enhance the learning, teaching and assessment of English worldwide. Its main funding partners are Cambridge University Press and Cambridge English Language Assessment and its aim is to create a 'profile' for English linked to the Common European Framework of Reference for Languages (CEF). English Profile outcomes, such as the English Vocabulary Profile, will provide detailed information about the language that learners can be expected to demonstrate at each CEF level, offering a clear benchmark for learners' proficiency. For more information, please visit www.englishprofile.org

Cambridge Dictionaries

Cambridge dictionaries are the world's most widely used dictionaries for learners of English. The dictionaries are available in print and online at dictionary.cambridge.org. Copyright © Cambridge University Press, reproduced with permission.

The publishers are grateful to the following for permission to reproduce copyright photographs and material:

T = Top, B = Below, L = Left, R = Right, C = Centre, B/G = Background

p.8 (T): ©patpitchaya/iStock/360/Getty Images; p.8 (1): ©Oleksiy Mark/iStock/360/Getty Images; p.8 (2): ©Ameng Wu/iStock /360/Getty Images; p.8 (3): ©Duygun VURAL/iStock/360/Getty Images; p.8 (4): ©hamurishi/iStock/360/Getty Images; p.8 (5): ©studionobra/iStock/360/Getty Images; p.8 (6): ©AleksVF/iStock/360/Getty Images; p.14 (TL): ©Joe McBride/Iconica/Getty Images; p.14 (TR): ©DAJ/Getty Images; p.14 (BL): ©Yvette Cardozo/Alamy; p.15 (T): ©bevangoldswain/iStock/360/Getty Images; p.15 (BL): ©Jose Luis Pelaez Inc/Shutterstock; p.15 (BR): ©Kovalchuk Oleksandr/Shutterstock; p.20 (L): ©Avatar_023/Shutterstock; p.20 (CL): ©PhotoAlto/Laurence Mouton/Brand X Pictures/Getty Images; p.20 (C): ©StockLite/Shutterstock; p.20 (CR): ©Patrick Breig/Shutterstock; p.20 (R): ©Denkou Images/Cultura/Getty Images; p. 21 (TL): ©Didecs/Shutterstock; p.21 (TR): ©IvonneW/iStock/360/Getty Images; p.21 (CL): ©vuvu/Shutterstock; p.21 (CR): ©Zoonar RF/Zoonar/360/Getty Images; p.21 (BL): ©Tatiana Popova/Shutterstock; p.21 (BR): ©Oleksiy Mark/iStock/360/Getty Images; p.22 (T): ©Radius/Superstock; p.22 (B): ©Hero Images/Getty Images; p.24: ©Fuse/Getty Images; p.26 (TL, BR): ©Eduardo Jose Bernardino/iStock/360/Getty Images; p.26 (TR): ©jodiejohnson/iStock/360/Getty Images; p.26 (BL): ©C. Diane O' Keefe/iStock/360/Getty Images; p.27: ©saras66/Shutterstock; p.31 (TL): ©Sergio Martinez/Shutterstock; p.31 (TC): ©ULKASTUDIO/Shutterstock; p.31 (TR): ©Nattika/Shutterstock; p.31 (CL): ©rimglow/iStock/360/Getty Images; p.31 (C): ©Bozena Fulawka/Shutterstock; p.31 (CR): ©Meelena/Shutterstock; p.31 (BL): ©Viktor1/Shutterstock; p.31 (BC): ©gmevi/iStock/360/Getty Images; p.31 (BR): ©voltan1/iStock/360/Getty Images; p.32 (TL): ©chengyuzheng/iStock/360/Getty Images; p.32 (TR): ©anankkml/iStock/360/Getty Images; p.32 (CL): ©Steve Lenz/iStock/360/Getty Images; p.32 (CR): ©Eric Isselée/iStock/360/Getty Images; p.32 (BL): ©xstockerx/Shutterstock; p.32 (BR): ©StockSolutions/iStock/360/Getty Images; p.33: ©killerbayer/iStock/360/Getty Images; p.34: ©Adam Hester/Corbis; p.40: ©Pankaj & Insy Shah/Getty Images; p. 42 (TL, BL): ©Vtls/Shutterstock; p.42 (TR, BR): ©White Smoke/Shutterstock; p.50 (T): ©epa/Corbis; p.50 (C): ©Ralf-Finn Hestoft/CORBIS; p.50 (B): ©AFP/Getty Images; p.51 (L): ©DenisKotr/iStock/360/Getty Images; p.51 (CL): ©Room27/Shutterstock; p.51 (C): ©Ad Oculos/Shutterstock; p.51 (CR): ©sagir/Shutterstock; p.51 (R): ©bopav/Shutterstock; p.55: ©AFP/Getty Images; p.58 (TR): ©UNITED ARTISTS/THE KOBAL COLLECTION; p.58 (TL): ©Pictorial Press Ltd/Alamy; p.58 (B): ©REX/Everett Collection; p.60: ©REX/Geoffrey Swaine; p.63: ©diego cervo/iStock/360/Getty Images

Cover photographs by: ©Yuliya Koldovska/Shutterstock; ©Lukasz Pajor/Shutterstock; ©William Perugini/Shutterstock.

The publishers are grateful to the following illustrators:

David Semple 5, 18, 20, 29, 37, 38, 39, 52; Fred Van Deelen (The Organisation) 7, 25, 62; Julian Mosedale 16, 19, 21, 31, 38, 42, 59

The publishers are grateful to the following contributors:

Blooberry Design Ltd: text design and layouts; Claire Parson: cover design; Hilary Fletcher: picture research; Leon Chambers: audio recordings; Karen Elliott: Pronunciation sections; Diane Nicholls: Get it right! exercises